D1595864

JOURNEY INTO CONTEMPLATION

George A. Maloney, S.J.

Cover: Robert Manning

Imprimi Potest: Rev. Vincent M. Cook, S.J.
  Provincial, New York Province, May 12, 1983

2483

Published by: Living Flame Press/Box 74/Locust
Valley, New York 11560.

IBSN: 0-914544-51-9

Dedication

To Elaine Blaettler
for all her invaluable help over the years.

Contents

Introduction

God is love *(1 Jn.4:8)*.

God's love is pure emptying . . . a self-giving that knows no end of surrender in order to share His very life with His human creatures.

If God, in the three persons of Father, Son and Holy Spirit, is always "toward" us in self-giving, are we not, therefore, called to experience God's triune, personalized love for us? This love is bursting all around us in the millions of creatures that shout out His loving presence.

The Good News that Jesus Christ came to reveal to us and make possible through His Spirit is that the Holy Trinity really lives within us through the gift of our Baptism. If such infinte, perfect love abounds in our hearts through the Spirit that is given to us *(Rm.5:5)*, why do you and I not experience this love daily, hourly, in this very moment?

I have found after Vatican II, a tremendous release of the Holy Spirit in the hearts of many Christians, especially the laity in the Catholic Church. Such persons desire ardently to pray in a more contemplative, experiential way rather than with the vocal and meditational forms of prayer traditionally taught them. Yet, many complain of the lack of spiritual guides and teachers to give adequate instruction concerning contemplative prayer. Many fear to leave the more secure forms of prayer in order to launch into a prayer that could easily lead them into error. However, they feel certain that God is calling them to a more immediate and direct encounter with Him through a silencing of their mental activities and a centering within themselves as the focus of their prayer.

It was in answer to such pleas for teachings on contemplative prayer that in April, 1982, I launched, under the auspices of our *Contemplative Ministries,* based in California, a monthly newsletter *called Inscape.* Once a month for ten months, I prepare a teaching on some aspect of contemplative prayer and the spiritual life, geared to those who are not beginners in prayer, but rather to those who have already led a disciplined prayer life for several years. In these teachings, I strive to combine our Catholic heritage from Scripture, the teachings of the Church and the writings of the spiritual masters from both the Christian East and West.

The response has been most encouraging from all across the country. I am, therefore, most grateful to Living Flame Press of Locust Valley, New York for publishing these first ten teachings in book form.

I offer them to you in the prayerful hope that they may help you, not only to meet God, the "Consuming Fire" *(Heb. 12:29),* but to form a contemplative prayer group. I encourage you to study these and other excellent teachings on prayer published by other authors. Share with each other the guidance of the Spirit that you recieve concerning such teachings, and ultimately, pray with others in a contemplative setting, thus discovering the God of love, experiencing His presence in a loving community.

George A. Maloney, S.J.

1

Are You Called to Be a Contemplative?

Do you often have a burning feeling deep down within you, a real hunger that nothing created on the face of the earth can ever satisfy? You can stretch out feverishly to possess money, power, sex, fame, health, beauty and yet you will return always to that inside hunger that only God can satisfy because He put it there. And that is because God created you and me "according to His image and likeness" *(Gn 1:26)*. He has locked deeply within your heart seeds of infinite growth to become His child by grace, just as His only begotten Son is by nature. You have been created to "become participator in God's nature" *(2 P 1:4)*. We all " . . . are the ones He chose especially long ago and intended to become true images of His Son, so that His son might be the eldest of many brothers" *(Rm 8:29)*.

Look at your life and see how you have changed your set of values that have guided your motivation in what you do and think and say. So many of us think wealth, honors, power can bring an end to that inner "sickness" that longs always for something greater than what we have or who we are. Perhaps it was learning or professional work or involvement in social causes that you thought could bring those inner yearnings to satisfying fulfillment. With King Solomon you can readily admit:

> I then reflected on all that my hands had achieved and on all the effort I had put into its achieving. What vanity it all is and chasing of the wind! *(Qo 2:11)*

For most of us, it takes several years of such futile searching to realize that nothing in the world can ever satisfy us but God. For it is God who has given us this basic drive to possess Him and to be possessed by Him. In the words of Francis Thompson in his *Hound of Heaven*, it is always a stretching out to possess the Unpossessable that makes all other possession vain. St. Augustine discovered that God alone was the ultimate answer to meaningful existence.

> "Too late have I loved Thee, O Thou, Beauty of ancient days, yet ever new! Too late I have loved Thee! And behold, Thou wert within and I abroad, and there I searched for Thee; deformed, I plunging amid those fair forms which Thou hast made. Thou wert with me, but I was not with Thee, which unless they were in Thee, were not at all."

GOD LOVES US INFINITELY

God is love. His presence as personalized relations of uncreated energies of love surrounds you, permeates you, bathes you constantly in His great loving communication of Himself. This is an on-going self-giving on the part of God the Father through His Son in His Spirit. Or rather, isn't it more that it is an on-going discovery on your part of how completely self-giving God is always toward you and how intimately close He is to you?

One of the great contemplatives in Christianity is St. Symeon the New Theologian (+ 1022). For him the important question that all of us must answer, through experience that will radically change our lives, is not whether the Trinity lives within us; it is whether we are consciously aware, through a penitential conversion that must be a continued process, that we live in the Father's love in Jesus Christ through the illumination of the Holy Spirit. If the presence of the Holy Trinity is living and operating within all of us, how is it possible that we are not consciously experiencing this reality? St. Symeon uses the rather earthy example of a pregnant woman. She is aware that new life stirs within her. No one from the outside needs to tell her of that inner reality. If the Christian possesses this divine light, how is it possible that he or she is not aware of this light and its effects in daily living?

DEGREES OF AWARENESS

You know in your human experiences of loving another human being that you have grown in awareness of that union with the one loved. You also know that your awareness of union with God dwelling within you can grow in intensity. But you must distinguish between faith, an infused gift of the Holy Spirit leading you into new depths

11

of conscious knowledge, and the effects in the affective order of an individual's psychological make-up, wherein there can be room for special charisms of mystical prayer as well as great self-deception. Hence, we ought to distinguish between true contemplation that can unfold gradually, even without great mystical gifts in the psychological, phenomenal order, and should be the continued growth of the Baptism of the Holy Spirit, and the extraordinary gifts in prayer that depend so much upon psychological preparation of nature and condition of life.

Did not Jesus Christ promise to all that the pure of heart would be blessed and would see God *(Mt 5:8)*? As Christians, in ancient times and in the 20th century, on Mount Athos and in the Bronx, have purified their hearts, they have entered into a contemplation of true realities unknown and unseen by others who do not pray deeply. In the deeper knowledge in which God communicates Himself to human beings more directly and immediately, Christians of deep prayer know, not through concepts, but by means of a direct "seeing" of God's revelation.

WHAT IS CONTEMPLATION?

But what then is contemplation? How does it differ from the basic prayer that you learned from childhood? In your oral or verbal saying of prayers or in a meditational type of "reasoned" prayer, you are the center of activity. God is conceived of as an "object" to which you direct your affectivity, your petitions, your sorrow, your deep gratitude for His kindnesses in His gifts given to you. Prayer, therefore, is that general art whereby you as a human being communicate with God in knowledge and love. You lift your mind and your heart toward God.

As you grow in human friendships from talking to a person outside of yourself to silencing of all your own self-centered words, ideas and desires, and ultimately to a union of self-surrender toward the other, so you move in prayer, not primarily to receive gifts from God, but to surrender yourself as a self-giving gift to Him who has given you everything in Jesus Christ. Prayer becomes more and more your avenue to enter into God's timeless and infinite, personal and perfect love for you individually. Prayer raises your consciousness to the primal experience that is the beginning and the end of all reality, namely your being grasped by God, known and loved uniquely by Him, so that, in such a re-creating experience, you rise to new levels of union and hence of spiritual perfection.

You enter into the land of contemplation when you move away from this or that act that you are in charge of to enter into a more total experience of oneness with God. God breaks through more immediately to you by His Spirit communicating to your "spirit", with your total self moving into a union with God. As you experience God by greater and greater infusion of faith, hope and love as gifts from the Holy Spirit, He is no longer in your awareness as someone outside of you only in His wondrous creations of nature or His studied perfections, but as also dwelling within you. Your response is one of more total self-surrendering love that pushes your consciousness of your new identity, your new *I-ness* in God's *Thou-ness*, to new heights.

Such an expansion of self-identity and inner nobility, due to God's personal love for you, is never content with one such prayerful experience. An inner dynamism, the indwelling Holy Spirit, drives you to continued and more intense relationship. The sameness and stability of your love for God fills you with a restless motion, a stretching-out quality toward God, the Unpossessable, that thrills you because you know that, try as you may, you can never exhaust this richness. Love always beckons you to partake of more of the joy that is already yours.

BORN FOR CONTEMPLATION

Contemplation, therefore, is basically a look turned toward God. It is you standing, as it were, outside of your habitual idea that you have had of yourself and of God and of others and of the whole world. It is getting down below that false everyday ego and getting into your deepest source where you stand before God, as you consciously turn toward your Source, your Origin. You can see that we are not dealing here with an exercise of piety alone. We are certainly not dealing with anything that is dependent upon perseverance in a certain method, a way of breathing or sitting or what have you. Contemplation is something applicable to every human being, and, therefore, should be as natural as a baby looking on its father's or mother's face.

You, as a Christian baptized into the very life of the Trinity, are called by Jesus Christ in His Spirit to enter into a consciousness of communing with the Holy Trinity that knows no interruption. As you grow in the Baptism of the Holy Spirit, you are to continue to grow in awareness of the greatest of all realities, that the Trinity dwells within you and loves you with an infinite, most intimate love. You are meant, by your Baptism and your living the Good News that Jesus preached, to yield yourself in each moment to the uncreated energies of God, Father, Son and Holy Spirit, divinizing you into a child of God. You are to become vitally aware at each moment that you are loved as a child by an infinitely loving Father.

In this there can be no distinction between laity and priests and religious. All are called to live consciously in Christ Jesus and obey His commands. All must hear His voice and follow Him. All too often, certain theologians in times past have accentuated the total gratuitousness of the gift of contemplation as God's gift to certain individuals living a certain style of life. They have distinguished between "acquired contemplation" and "infused contemplation." By doing certain things a person could "acquire" some type or level of contemplation. But only a very few privileged souls have received infused contemplation, which such theologians describe in terms of extraordinary psychic manifestations in prayer.

Infused contemplation was supposed to be real mysticism, a sheer gift, not given to everyone but only to very special persons as a special call. The stages that described the level of mysticism attained were called: Prayer of Quiet, Full Union, Ecstatic Union and Spiritual Marriage. Often certain mystical gifts were manifested in these stages and hence a distinction was made between the "concomitant phenomena" and "charismatic phenomena" of infused contemplation. The first set of gifts was centered around the gifts of the Spirit, especially wisdom and knowledge, deep inward peace, joy, love and the obscure sense of God's presence. The charismatic phenomena were visions, ESP powers such as telepathy, clairvoyance, levitation, psychokinesis etc., trances, locutions and ecstasies. These were not considered essential and could be found outside Christianity.

Several modern theologians, such as Karl Rahner, join the Greek Fathers of the early Chuch to dispute such a distinction between acquired and infused contemplation. For them all grace is "special," being in essence the self-communication of God. Rahner thus writes:

> Mysticism . . . occurs within the framework of normal graces and within the experience of faith. To this extent, those who insist that mystical experience is not specifically different from the ordinary life of grace (as such) are certainly right.

STAGES OF PRAYER

The beginning stage in prayer, as in the unfolding of a human friendship, is a prayer of simple reflection. When anyone in a friendship starts to know another extrinsically, he or she does not immediately plumb the depths of the other person. Deep communion evolves through years of coming to know the person with one's mind and intellect, as well as with the senses. Gradually faith and trust are built up, so that one can be admitted into the inner sanctuary of the other's being.

In Christian prayer there is always a need for ordering the truths of faith. You begin with a method of "meditation" that enables you to reflect, ponder, measure, compare and organize. Here the basic activity revolves around the use of your own intellect and reasoning process on the matters of faith. We ought to distinguish here between this usual sense of meditation with our discursive reasoning and the use of the term "meditation" as used in *TM* or other (even Christian) forms of transcendental meditation or centering prayer that go beyond any discursive reasoning.

In the beginning stage of meditational prayer, the basic activity revolves around the use of your own intellect and reasoning process on the matters of faith. This activity moves one to affections, toward the union to feel, to touch the spiritual reality about which one is meditating. In a discursive manner, you may meditate on the Trinity, but always each mental activity is a preparatory step toward a living experience of the Trinity, not as a concept, but as the living God abiding withing you.

This is the level at which you delve into Scripture and come to make contact with God through "meditating" or concentrating on revealed truth found in Scripture or on some scene from the Bible that will mediate to you the presence of the living God.

As the Holy Spirit infuses gifts of faith, hope and love as you become more affectively present to

God through the use of your imagination, memory, understanding and will, you are able to move from the given biblical text to the presence of God and His divine action in your very being and life. This is the second stage of development in prayer-consciousness and is characterized by intense affections that surge up with ardent longings to be more intimately united with Jesus and the Heavenly Father. Many consolations are found in this second stage of your prayer life. God seems to be everywhere, even outside of your period of concentrated prayer alone with Him. Your daily living takes on an "affective" finding of God in places and persons where you had never before "seen" Him.

As you learn to yield your aggressive activity both in prayer and in your daily actions, gentleness and docility to the indwelling presence of God take over in your prayer life. There is a "letting go" of your own powers. A new sensitivity, a new listening to God's presence and loving activity within you and around you appears. You seem to be living on a new plateau of awareness of God's presence. The Holy Spirit has poured into your heart deeper infusions of faith, hope and love so that whether you find yourself in ardent consolation or aridity, there seems to be a deep peace and joy. An inner awareness that God is present is now yours by a new way of knowing that has not come from your own rational powers but from the Holy Spirit. This is the beginning stage of contemplation that we could call the prayer of faith or the prayer of the heart.

In the second book of his *Ascent to Mount Carmel,* St. John of the Cross describes this transitional prayer, leaving the discursive type of prayer or meditation to enter into contemplation:

> "The third and surest sign is that a person likes to remain alone in loving awareness of God, without particular considerations, in interior peace and quiet and repose, and without the acts and exercises (at least discursive, those in which one progresses from point to point) of the intellect, memory and will; and that he prefers to remain only in the general, loving awareness and knowledge we mentioned, without any particular knowledge or understanding."

The whole world now becomes a diaphanous presence of God's love, shining through to you. No longer do you find one world that is somehow sacred and a different world that is profane. You move, not as an angel ignoring this world around you; rather you see the world now in all its uniqueness, and yet precisely that uniqueness is discovered in the finality of God's creative love.

You have entered into true freedom. No longer do you see blindly merely in the light of your own world built up by your desires and projections. You have died to yourself and now you are alive to Jesus Christ. You seek to live according to the Father's *Logos* found in each situation. Through deep faith, you see Christ everywhere. It is already a share in the vision that will be face-to-face in Heaven; the substance of God's immense love is already encountered in each moment made manifest through His Word Incarnate, Jesus Christ. The world is now being transfigured by the presence and power of God in all things. You realize now that you are called by Him to be a reconciler of the whole world, as St. Paul writes *[2 Co 5:18]*. The earth is already filled with God's glory and you are privileged to see part of it, depending on the purification to which you submit—the dying to self.

TRUE TEST OF AUTHENTIC CONTEMPLATION

Many Christians who would aspire to deeper contemplative prayer may forget that such a surrender to the indwelling Word of God is a definite call to live seriously at every moment one's Baptism and the message of Christ that death is truly resurrection. This death is dying to self-centeredness and living in love according to the movement of the Spirit of the risen Lord. If one thinks being a contemplative in such a hidden life is egotistic and easy, then that one has not lived such a life to its fullest. God is calling you to be a contemplative in this sense: to love the Lord your God with your whole heart, your whole soul, your whole mind, your whole strength—this is to be a contemplative, to look at God as the root of your being and to love him in all things.

God calls you to love, and, now on earth as later in Heaven, you are to spend your eternity growing in the love of God as mirrored in other beings. Heaven is going to be this whole wonderful world transfigured by the presence of God through an ever-increasing degree of consciousness of His presence and love.

You can test whether God has really brought you to a true experience of contemplating the indwelling Trinity by your ability to go out and love others as God has loved you. The contemplative sees him/herself as a person loved by God very much, and in this grace he/she discovers him/herself more centered upon God, more one with God, and yet more one with all other beings. This is contemplation—a gift of God's loving presence within you so strongly felt that you can find God everywhere and praise Him in union with all the living and the dead.

It is answering God's clarion call for you to become totally alive to God and God to you, as you live each moment bathed in the wonder and beauty of His eternal light. Immersed in that light you open up to the fullness of Total Love for which you were created. It is you, as unique creature, responding to your Creator. You have spoken your "fiat" to your Beloved's call, and your Beloved responds to you. Absolute Love overflows from within you, pouring forth in all its abundant richness to the whole created world!

"Anyone who loves me will be true to my word, and my father will love him; we will come to him and make our dwelling place with him."   *(Jn 14:23)*

2

How to Form and Develop a Contemplative Prayer Group

I continually hear the desperate cry: "Teach me how to pray in a contemplative manner. What must I do that I am not doing now? Is there a special way of doing it? Do you have any practical techniques that will help me to become a contemplative?"

I would like to make some very practical suggestions on how to do it, namely, how to form and develop a contemplative prayer-group. But the reader must have clearly in mind the interrelationships between material aids, techniques in prayer and the free gift of God's presence through the infusion of His Holy Spirit in the gifts of faith, hope and love.

Some bodily and psychic aids can be of great help in entering into a deeper awareness of God's presence that is always an abiding sameness of infinite love. We are "whole" persons when we enter into prayer—persons of body, soul and spirit. It is only natural that material aids can help us to move from one level to another in a fuller integration of our total human nature in order to pray more completely as individuals meeting our unique, personalized God. We are in need of signs and symbols drawn from our experience in the world. Such signs as light, darkness, fire and breath are perceived as filled with spiritual meaning and they act on our consciousness.

We should, therefore, not be in fear of such techniques if they truly do help us to pray better. Christians down through the centuries have always used them. They learned that we all have to quiet our inner, psychic world and this can be done easily by rhythmic breathing and other centering techniques. But there are some important principles to keep in mind:

1. God wishes to give Himself to us directly through an immediate experience. This communication is made to us as whole human beings. We need to prepare ourselves through asceticism and psychosomatic techniques.

2. Yet these are means; God's grace is a sheer gift. Let us explore this group technique as a means given to us by God.

DEVELOPING A CONTEMPLATIVE PRAYER GROUP

As you and many others are encouraged more and more to pursue your God-given desire for a deeper, more contemplative prayer-life, you find that you have a strong need to share that desire with others. This need can be met by urging such persons to form themselves with you into intimately loving and sharing groups. An individual, praying in a contemplative manner, has continued need of a support group and proper spiritual guidance. I am convinced that the Holy Spirit will guide such sincere persons, but usually in the context of a small, intimate, loving group of persons deeply committed to study, share and pray together. Discernment will be found in prayer as all the members of this small group seek in love to help each other grow. There is also the need for such groups to be in touch with the discernment that derives from the Church's traditions and teachings about prayer. Many tools are available for contemplative prayer groups, such as the numerous excellent books and tapes by outstanding spiritual teachers throughout the world. These tools help such groups to be in touch with the total Church in its guidance and encouragement toward a deeper prayer-life.

The aims of such a group of individuals seriously committed in love and service to each other can be primarily:

1. To build each other up by mutual study, sharing and praying over teachings given through books and tapes that deal with the spiritual life.

2. Mutually to share your faith vision with others; above all, to be a healing and loving listener to the others in the group.

3. To assist in the process of listening to the main spiritual director of the group, the Holy Spirit, and help in the discernment for the group and the individuals in the group.

4. Above all, to pray and worship together as a group, especially in silent, contemplative prayer.

I would like to share a letter sent to me which describes how a "Martha and Mary Group" developed and how it functions.

"Two and a half years ago, a friend and I discovered the need to draw away from the world once a week to share on a spiritual level, to pray and meditate together.

We found another friend to join us and this "trinity" began weekly to get together. As the months passed, other women expressed a desire to join us. Some did for a time and then dropped away because the type of prayer we were experiencing was too demanding for them. Others have remained faithful to the weekly commitment.

We never number more than seven and we feel that this aids us greatly in sharing on a deep, spiritual level in such a small, intimate group. As time passed and we grew spiritually, we introduced disciplines to help us remain constant toward our prime purpose in coming together once a week.

One of the first aids in keeping up a disciplined seriousness when we came together was to eliminate the coffee and cake social that gradually developed after our meeting. We found that we at times lapsed into "holy gossip" and it set a bad tone for the rest of the day. Now the entire hour and a half is devoted strictly to things spiritual.

We meet on Monday which in the Eastern Church is the day devoted to the Holy Angels. We count very much on angelic protection because we have realized for a long time that we were involved in a spiritual warfare against inimical forces.

We also try to begin each Monday by attending Mass in our parishes and/or by being silent and prayerful until meeting time. In this way, we come together in a quieted state of love.

A priest-friend suggested for variety that we

meet on the first Monday of each month at the beach or in a park or a chapel. This way our meetings do not become stagnant. We have adopted this practice and have found it most helpful.

We open our group to any woman seeking a supportive group that turns away from the noisy, "worldly" world. We have no structure other than a simple format to prevent ourselves from going off into tangents.

Each member is responsible for holding a meeting in her home. When she does, she prepares the program of prayer, instruction and ends with a Christian meditation set to music.

Other women, who would like to be a part of our prayer-group but cannot attend our meetings because of work or other responsibilities feel close to us and ask to be remembered in our prayers as they phone in to us their requests.

A second "Martha and Mary Group" has recently formed in Seattle, WA. and we pray and share with them. We hope they will share in the many blessings the Lord has showered down upon us in our contemplative prayer-group."

FORMAT

The format that a given meeting will observe will depend greatly upon the maturity and the needs of the group. Basically, the membership should be made up of like-minded persons who are more or less on a similar level of the spiritual life. A serious commitment should be made by each member to the group and a time and place chosen that will be convenient for all. The size could be from two members to twelve. Beyond this number of members intimacy fades off into impersonalism.

The setting for the meeting should be a quiet, carpeted room. Cushions should be available for those who prefer to sit on the floor, to have the sense of literally being "grounded" in the Lord. For the others, chairs with straight backs should be available, so that the members can form a circle. Members should move into the appointed place when all have arrived, and there enter into a deep sense of quiet and peaceful presence to God among them.

TECHNIQUES

If we claim to be true Christians, we must live the incarnational religion of Jesus Christ. Matter, as God creates it, is good. It can, therefore, especially since the Incarnation, become a meeting place with the Divine. We cannot ignore the material world around us, especially the fact that we are made up of matter.

The Anglicans, Catholics and Orthodox have always maintained a healthy use of material techniques in their prayer-life: bodily gestures, the use of singing and music, dance, use of bread and wine, oil, holy water, touch in healing, use of candles etc. Should we, therefore, fear techniques for becoming quieted, techniques that we can find employed by all humans, regardless of country and religion?

Therefore, the coming together as a group can be facilitated to reach that inward stillness by encouraging each of the members to select the position or posture for prayer, listening and sharing that is most conducive to him/her for concentration and listening to the indwelling presence of the Holy Spirit. Some may prefer to sit on cushions in the *lotus* or *semi-lotus* position or any other simple sitting posture on the floor while still others may prefer to sit upon the straight back chair.

Centering prayer techniques that combine rhythmic breathing with the use of a *mantra* or Christian phrase, especially the name of Jesus, can be very effective in bringing the entire group to God, their Center. Perhaps a burning candle might be placed in the center with some flowers. Soft uplifting music can be used in the background to silence the hearts of the members as they become recollected as a group.

We should always keep in mind that techniques are never in themselves prayer but can be powerful aids to center us and silence our distracted minds and hearts so that we can pray with greater concentration and a fuller consciousness of God's loving presence. The ultimate worth of any technique must be measured by the fruit produced. A technique has no meaning unless we ask the question: "How is it being used by me? What are the fruits that come from such use? Does it help me and the other members in the group to pray with greater consciousness of the centrality of God among us?"

STUDY-TIME

Study about the literature and teachings of Christian spiritual leaders from the past to the present is an important part of a community bonded together in love to be guided by the Spirit. That Spirit operates in like manner in your life as He has operated in the lives of earlier Christians.

There are some very definite principles in the spiritual life that must not only be studied by serious-minded Christians but must be applied to their daily living.

St. Paul exhorts Christians to such a serious study. "Finally brothers, fill your minds with everything that is true, everything that is noble, everything that is good and pure, everything that we love and honor, and everything that can be thought virtuous or worthy of praise" *(Ph 4:8)*. Study allows us to change our negative habits of thought and replace them with a renewing of the mind *(Rm 12:2)*. Through studying the teachings of Spirit-filled instructors, we can share in the Spirit's guidance and thus prevent ourselves from falling into error. This is so very important in the area of contemplative prayer.

In any given period of study, whether it is done communally in your prayer-group or individually, there are four steps that are important to ensure serious and successful study.

1. *Repetition* is a way of re-fashioning a new thought pattern or an insight. Have you ever noticed how often in TV commericals a given brand name is repeated? Repetition is the mother of learning. It would be good for the members of your prayer-group to know in advance what will be the topic to be studied during the next meeting. If it is a definite material to be gone over, such as a chapter from an author's book or a tape, efforts should be made to provide members of the prayer-group with such material in advance of the meeting.

2. *Concentration* both in private and in communal study is most necessary in order that the attention

of the individual may be completely centered on the given topic. Centering prayer in deep quiet before the study part of a meeting will be a great help, as also will be the general tenor of quiet and peace maintained throughout the meeting.

3. *Comprehension* brings the truth contained in the teaching into your intellectual grasp. It unfolds in greater insights and applications that will come forth in the sharing segment of the meeting. Such richness will then be brought into your daily living, but all depending on the degree of your comprehension.

4. *Reflection* is demanded even during the period of study. This reflection pushes you to connect things you already have studied and made a part of your life with what you are now studying. In a Christian prayer-group it is important to reflect in order to see the studied material in the light of God's revealed truth. Reflection calls for humility as we place ourselves in the attitude of students eager to acquire new knowledge, to admit before others and, above all, God, that there is so much more to learn, and to enrich our lives with these new truths.

Concretely, when it is time to move into the study portion of the meeting, the one in charge can carefully go over the topic, either by reading what it is hoped the members have already read thoroughly at home or by playing a tape of a highly respected spiritual teacher. Persons can take notes on insights discovered in the reading or applications to their own personal life or the tenor of that prayer-group.

SHARING ONE'S FAITH

Your reaction to the study portion of the meeting should lead you and the other members to want to share your faith-experiences as they touch the matter discussed. This takes humility, courage and love that builds up the Body of Christ. Here the one in charge of the meeting must have presence of mind and discretion to keep any member from monopolizing the sharing; above all, from turning the period into a selfish aggrandizement or "ego-trip."

Such sharing is given as briefly as possible with humility and sincerity and, of course, let it be pertinent to the material at hand!

SILENT PRAYER

A good period of time, at least one half-hour of silent prayer, should be the climax of the meeting. Let the members again become centered on the indwelling Trinity through the use of the techniques earlier discussed. Soft music can be used if the group through experience finds it helpful. Usually the majority, from my own observations, prefer complete silence at this time.

In contemplative prayer, the accent is not on your doing through the use of your discursive powers of memory, imagination, understanding and will. The purpose of the period of study and sharing has brought the members of the group to the "still-point" where the Holy Spirit comes to the rescue when you do not know how to pray as you ought *(Rm 8:26-27)*. It would be good to fix your attention on the indwelling Trinity by using a mantra as you mentally speak it softly within and synchronize it with your breathing. Let even good thoughts pass through your consciousness as you gently move closer to God, your Center. Do not be anxious to "think." You have done enough of that. Rest in the truth studied. Let it be the water in which you swim. Do not worry about mental images. Let go of all thoughts and images and merely maintain an inner attitude of complete, open receptivity to God's in-filling presence. You seek to remain fixed through faith, hope and love upon God's loving presence as Father, Son and Spirit within you. Move gently away from your rational "speaking" to God through ideas, feelings, images to remain humbly on a meta-rational listening level as God speaks His word to you through His Holy Spirit.

INTERCESSORY PRAYER

The final section, as the participants come out of their silent oneness with God and each other, should be a period of intercessory prayer for the individual needs of the members, their families and friends and the needs of human beings throughout the world. This facilitates a return to a larger experience of Church and of the world.

SPIRITUAL DIRECTION IN A GROUP

Some spiritual leaders are practising spiritual direction given within the cntext of a group. Tilden H. Edwards in his book: *Spiritual Friend* develops this type of spiritual direction. I am not proposing spiritual direction as the primary scope of your coming together in a prayer-group. I would rather emphasize that all members, being aware of the movement of the Holy Spirit during the meeting, can act as vehicles of the guidance of the Spirit for the needs of the group, as well as those of each individual.

Fr. Shaun McCarty in an article describes some of the benefits of group direction and discernment. Some benefits that accrue to the group and its individual members are: freedom from the danger of dependency on only one director: avoidance of undue influences by one person upon another; a greater richness through diversity and the possibility of being affected by other people's prayer; easier communication for some who have difficulty in relating one-to-one; the benefits of communal experience; the impetus of a group accountability. Some possible disadvantages might be: the lessening of individual accountability through hiding within the group; some members not truly open to the Spirit perhaps making judgments with a "carnal mind;" the difficulty of self-disclosure in a group for some.

Let us be aware of the healing that comes in a prayer-group when individuals follow St. James' instruction: "So confess your sins to one another, and pray for one another and this will cure you" (Ja 5:16).

When we come together, we are first a sinful people. By acknowledging this in a group both communally and individually, we become freed to hear the unconditional call of God's love and open ourselves to great inner healing. Such healing can be extended by the members to an individual of the group by actually laying hands on a fellow-member in need and praying for healing of body, soul and spirit.

AN "UPPER ROOM"

As Christians living in the world today, we all need an "upper room" where we can join together in prayer. Such "an upper room" community established for your contemplative prayer group's use, will fill a need not only for you to pray together, but to build a community of close, personal relationships founded on the love of God and each other. As Mary and the Apostles gathered together after the Ascension of Jesus, so too we need to come into a "special place" to set aside time to be still and know that He is God. We need to listen to the sound of the "strong driving wind" of the Spirit, so that we can become open vessels, receptive to the infilling of His Spirit of love.

"After that they returned to Jerusalem from the mount called Olivet near Jerusalem—a mere sabbath's journey away. Entering the city, they went to the upstairs room where they were staying. Together, they devoted themselves to constant prayer. There were some women in their company, and Mary the Mother of Jesus, and his brothers."
(Acts 1:12-1)

3

Difficulties in Contemplation

God, through Jesus Christ, has called you not only to know the mysteries of His trinitarian family, but also to experience His inter-mutual love of Father, Son and Spirit for each of us. You are called to experience the ecstatic happiness of the Trinity. This joyful, exuberant, outpouring love of the Father through His Son, Jesus Christ, in His Spirit is to be a process of continued experiential growth reflected by our happy, self-giving, intimate love toward those whom we are called to love and serve.

The authentic test of how intimately you are living in God's presence is how intimately you are ready to live for others. The transformation of yourself into oneness with God can come about only through a mutual transformation into oneness with other human beings whom you are lovingly privileged to serve. Your dignity and the measure of sanctity of your life in God is shown by your striving to release God's loving presence in the world; the world in which you find yourself. Only in that time and space of our human situation with all its brokenness, banality and even sordidness will you discover God's love as transforming all things into a sharing of Himself.

You may be experiencing this brokenness in contemplation. Frequently, many complain about dryness, distractions and other areas of difficulties that could put an end to their efforts to pray. Let us look at this important area of your prayer-life, both the positive and negative elements, as well as some possible solutions and aids.

DIFFICULTIES IN CONTEMPLATIVE PRAYER

I have described contemplation as an habitual prayer attitude in which you move away from this or that act of which you are in charge to enter into a more total experience of oneness with God. God breaks through more immediately to you by His Spirit communicating to your "spirit", your total self moving into a union with God. As you experience God by greater and greater infusion of faith, hope and love as gifts from the Holy Spirit, He is no longer in your awareness as someone outside of you in His wondrous creations of nature or His studied perfections, but as dwelling within you. Your response is one of more total self-surrendering love that pushes your consciousness of your new identity, your new *I-ness* in God's *Thou-ness*, to new heights.

As you move into this simple presence of Jesus Christ, there is a great peace and quietude. In the beginning stages of "resting" in His presence, often intense affections may surge up with ardent longings to be more intimately united with Him and the Heavenly Father. The consolations in this period of your prayer life can be strong and attrative. God seems to be everywhere, even outside of your concentrated prayer alone with God. A global presence of Jesus Christ surrounds you and you begin to find Him in the world around you, in places and persons where you had never "seen" Him before.

A LETTING GO

You begin to yield with greater susceptibility to His loving presence. Your aggressive activity both in prayer and in your daily actions takes on a gentleness and docility to the indwelling presence of God, both within yourself and within all of creation around you. There is a "letting go" of your own controlled power and a new sensitivity develops, a new listening to God's presence and loving activity around you and within you. You seem to be living on a new plateau of awareness of God's presence.

He can seemingly do anything He wishes with you. Whether there is now ardent consolation or plain old dryness, there always seems to be a deep peace and joy in events which formerly were disturbing. Now they do not seem to disturb you.

The sensible presence of God in prayer has passed. As you continue walking along the paths of deeper prayer, eager for greater union with God, you no longer find that sweet presence of God. It is as if you have lost Him. The *Song of Songs* describes your experience in prayer:

"On my bed, at night, I sought him whom my heart loves.
I sought but did not find him . . .

I will seek him whom my heart loves.

. . . I sought but did not find him.

The watchmen came upon me on their rounds in the City:

"Have you seen him whom my heart loves?"

(Sg 3:1-3).

A CLEANSING DARKNESS

A new presence of God indwelling within you shows itself as darkness. There are no longer clear and distinct ideas about God. Rarely are you aware of moving from one affection to another in the course of your prayer. You have a dull sense of alienation as you seem to enter deeply within yourself. You see your own abyss of nothingness before the mountain of God's majesty. There is a feeling of self-dread with a crying out in urgency for the face of God. You wonder whether you have sinned and God has left you to yourself. Faith is deepening without the props of sensible consolation, images, words. The more you advance into this darkness, the more names about God and His attributes make no sense.

Nothing satisfies you. The very presence of God that had flooded you both in deep affective prayer and in contact with the world now seems utterly absent. God creates this necessary pruning, this dying of the seed in order that greater union with Him may become possible. You enter into a necessary dying to your self-reliance and a deepening of faith that only comes when you are in this darkness, standing before a wall that is impermeable by your own intellectual powers.

It is a crying out for God to show Himself in the night of the desert, where you understand your own absolute nothingness before God. There is a silencing of your own powers like the silence of steel in the black night. Only a person who has experienced this trial can understand because God has been all to this person. And now you have to dig roots and cry out in deep, dark, stark faith for the mercy of God: "Lord, Jesus Christ, have mercy on me!"

You should remember that, as you do not abandon yourself completely to God in a given moment and have it remain a fixed state of abandonment for the rest of your life, so entering into the state of contemplation and way of purer faith does not happen in one given moment, never to return to meditation. At times meditation will be possible and even desirable. At other times reading a few prayers at the beginning to "localize"yourself before God's majesty may be helpful. The use of the *Jesus Prayer* or some other "mantra" can be an excellent means of centering yourself before the presence of God.

DISCOURAGEMENT

It is in these beginning stages of entering into the dark desert of contemplation that many Christians become discouraged and give up moving deeper into non-mental prayer. Such discouragement can take many forms and can lead to many other problems in your prayer-life. You can readily understand why you must be constantly on your guard to fight discouragement in prayer. We are dealing with a relationship between ourselves and God in the related atmosphere of deeper faith.

Such a state of remaining concentrated in faith,

hope and love before God without any images, words or feelings is hardly a state "natural" to us, at least for most of our life before this stage has been reached in prayer. We are born with a tendency to take charge of our lives, to make decisions with ourselves as the center of focus, not God. To go to prayer daily and seek constantly to surrender in faith to the loving presence of God whom we cannot see with our senses is a wearing process that tears down our bodies and brings discouragement to our minds.

But discouragement often can come from our lack of inner discipline, from sloth, from self-centeredness, all of which, in the beginning stages of prayer, seek things such as consolations and insights from God. Little by little we slack off in our efforts to prepare ourselves for our daily encounter with the living God of Abraham, Isaac and Jacob. With little "success," judged from our own selfish criteria, we fall victim to discouragement and often cut down on our prayer-time, if we do not completely give it up.

You may have doubts in such a simplified prayer of faith that you are really praying at all. There are few concrete acts to fall back upon to give you some assurance that you are accomplishing anything or that you really are not wasting your time in harmful emptiness. Yet your activity consists precisely now in pushing your will to become more united in deeper faith, hope and love with that of God, even though there may be extreme dryness and even harmless distractions that cannot be avoided. It is to be expected, as you stop using your discursive powers of intellect, will and imagination, that there will be much wandering of these faculties in search of images and ideas upon which to feed.

A NEGATIVE ELEMENT

Such a prayer of faith has a negative element of slowing down the use of these faculties. A definite purgation process takes place. Even though the thought of God does not necessarily bring any consolation, faith is being exercised in a new way, freed from any ideas or words. The most evident purgation takes place in what St. John of the Cross describes: "Since God puts a soul in this dark night in order to dry up and purge its sensory appetite, He does not allow it to find sweetness or delight in anything."

We must actively intensify our activities and reflections on our daily living to check whether there are any sinful attachments or imperfections that are possibly at the root of such dryness. Abandonment to God in contemplation avoids the errors of Quietism that so wrongly gave up all activity on the part of the contemplative, especially in the area of self-examination. Such erroneous teaching held that true abandonment meant abandonment of self-activity and that sinful actions committed in such a state of deep, faithful abandonment would not be true sins.

The true *apophatic* (negative) theology of the Eastern Fathers is best expressed in the classical work of Pseudo-Dionysius of the 6th century who describes the knowing by unknowing:

"... and then it (God's presence in darkness) breaks forth, even from the things that are beheld and from those that behold them, and plunges the true initiate

into the Darkness of unknowing wherein he re-
nounces all the apprehensions of his understanding
and is enwrapped in that which is wholly intangible
and invisible, belonging wholly to Him that is
beyond all things and to none else (whether himself
or another), and being through the passive stillness
of all his reasoning powers united by his highest
faculty to Him that is Unknowable of whom thus by
a rejection of all knowledge he possesses a knowledge that exceeds his understanding."

POSITIVE ELEMENT

Even though there seemingly is a negative
presence of God to your senses, especially to your
discursive faculties, there is however an inex-
plicable sense of the presence of God in a new and
more hidden, yet more direct and immediate,
manner. This is the work of the Holy Spirit pouring into your being a deeper infusion of faith by
which you can "see" God. Leonard Boase describes this as a "sixth sense."

"It is a communion with God in which the soul is
aware of His reality and of His presence by a sort of
'sixth-sense' or 'second-sight' or 'telepathy' which is
specifically different from the kind of certainty that
He exists attained by logical demonstration. It is a
certainty different also from the assent of faith given
by Christians in every day conditions; but it differs
from this not specifically, but only because that
same certainty of faith has moved, so to speak, into
the sensitive focus of consciousness."

You can see how your life can change as your
prayer moves into purer faith. God becomes the

center of your life and all your striving. You praise God, not because He is good to you; but an increase of faith and hope and love now allows you to praise Him in every event, whether it be pleasant or unpleasant; whether in prayer you are bathed in consolation or desolation. In all things you praise Him because you desire to do so since God is desired, not for what He can do for you, but sheerly because He is goodness in Himself and infinitely loving.

DISTRACTIONS

Distractions are anything on a body, soul or spirit level that enters into your communication and communion with God. Voluntarily or involuntarily willed by you, they can prevent you from being attentive in faith, hope and love to God. Distractions tend to dissipate your attention to God and therefore defeat the prime purpose of prayer: to lift your mind and heart up to God in loving surrender and adoration.

Most distractions are considered by spiritual writers as involuntary and arise from your mental concentration in praying to God in faith. You can see how you experience distractions in most of your mental work, even outside of formal prayer-activity. Your mind is racing at a very rapid rate of brainwave activity as you employ your imagination and understanding to make contact with God. As you move away from discursive prayer, all the more should you expect your mind to invite distractions.

This state of deeper faith-prayer invites distractions especially from the psychic material that has been stored up in your unconscious for years. You would be naive, knowing the laws of nature, not to agree that there would be many thoughts, like idle reveries, dreaming aloud, even sexual feelings that could distract you from prayer by influencing the entire body powerfully.

Distractions can come also from outside of yourself. Atmospheric conditions can affect your body and mind, setting up distracting thoughts that make it difficult to focus upon God in prayer. Noises around you, in church or in your room when you pray, can often disturb you and take you away from adoring God.

Involuntary distractions can never in themselves take you away from centering upon God. They cannot touch your will to surrender in love to Him. The secret is not to fight such a distraction with a mental turning toward it which compounds the distraction by taking you even further from prayer.

Voluntary distractions in prayer, something that you freely and deliberately focus upon with attention, seem like contradictions in prayer; for either we want to pray or we don't. If we want to be attentive to something else, then evidently we do not want to be attentive to God. Prayer ceases when we sincerely no longer wish to communicate with God in loving adoration.

SOME HELPS

1. One help that can cut down on the involuntary distractions in prayer is your immediate preparation as you enter into prayer. Seek to be reverent in prayer, controlling your external senses, placing your body in a relaxed but prayerful attitude.
2. Make a purifying intention as to what you are

about to do in prayer. You wish in spite of any distractions to adore God and to be "present" in loving surrender to His majesty.

3. When involuntary distractions seemingly carry you away from the focus of God, gently but firmly move back into the faith orbit by centering upon God's presence. Often you can gently turn the distraction toward God in a plea of humility and of trust in Him to come to your assistance.

4. Often the ejaculation of the name of Jesus or some other simple form of God's name, when uttered with childlike love, will be sufficient to bring you back to God's presence.

5. Many of your distractions will arise unconsciously from your deep concern about your daily work or some plaguing worry. If such thoughts and worries haunt you during your prayer-period, it is often good to turn to a different form of prayer, one that engages your senses and mental faculties more fully. Reading a prayer slowly or a passage from Scripture or even making the worry itself the subject of a surrendering act of prayer can often make a difference.

DRYNESS

I have already touched briefly on this topic of dryness. It is a state in which your former sensible and spiritual consolations, the affections experienced in prayer before, seem to have disappeared. In varying intensity dryness seems to be a dark cloud that covers the light of God's presence.

Let us touch on dryness that results from your deliberate negligence, remotely or proximately, toward putting God at the center of your life.

Dom Belorgey, OCSO, distinguishes between *obscurity* and *vagueness*. In obscurity you truly desire to pray in spite of complete darkness and dryness. You stretch out in will to embrace God and to surrender to Him, even though He does not seem to be present.

But in *vagueness*, even though psychologically there is the same dryness and apparent absence of God, you yield to mental wanderings, reveries. You give up desiring to stretch out in darkness to possess God. Instead you yield to a void feeling. You remain locked inside of nothingness. You do not desire to push beyond by faith in total surrender to God.

Vagueness shows itself during the day's activities. Where your treasure is, there is your heart or your consciousness. If you do not have a desire to seek God during your activities throughout the day, such a lack of inner attentiveness will return in prayer. When over a long period of such infidelity to God you catch yourself and wish to return in fervor to God in prayer, it is advised that you return to a level of prayer that will involve your self again in a faith presence to God, even if this means to return to discursive prayer or to reading prayers. Learn to live with obscurity but avoid vagueness.

Allowing God to do with you what He wills through this dryness, discouragement and darkness is allowing yourself to become a pilgrim in the desert. The desert seems to be an endless waste, an expanse without water and nourishment. But you as pilgrim find a watering hole, an "oasis" in your journey as you immerse yourself through prayer into oneness with your God. You are not lost in aridity but are "found" in new life when through your brokenness you let go of the control you exercise over God and move into contemplative prayer through deeper faith, hope and love.

4

Discipline as an Aid to Prayer

There is a fundamental law in nature that could be formulated in these words: "There is nothing that lives but that something must die. There is nothing that dies but that something else will live." Jesus Christ taught this law many times in quite blunt language. He had seen in His growing years in Nazareth the sower that sowed seed in spring. And so He taught: "Unless a wheat grain falls on the ground and dies, it remains only a single grain; but if it dies, it yields a rich harvest. Anyone who loves his life loses it; anyone who hates his life in this world will keep it for the eternal life" *(Jn 12:24-25)*.

In paradoxical language Jesus insisted that if anyone wanted to be His disciple and obtain eternal life (live in the indwelling, trinitarian life), he had to begin by a "dying" process. He had to enter into a suffering, but one that would deliver him unto new life. He had to take the risk of surrendering himself to Him by giving up a lower level of existence which allowed him to be in dominance, ruling his own life, in order to accept

Christ's offer to move into a higher level of existence to be guided by His Holy Spirit.

PRAYER DEMANDS DISCIPLINE

I have often said that the two words most misunderstood by many Christians are *mysticism* and *asceticism*. You are beginning to understand contemplative life no longer as a rare state for rarefied individuals but as the call God gives to all His children to live ever more consciously in His love and to return that experienced love to other human beings. It is imperative that you understand the necessity of discipline if you are to attain any degree of intimate union in prayer with God and neighbor.

No doubt you see in the young generation the inroads that materialism and affluence have made, rendering them very self-centered individuals. Without discipline, no student can ever master any subject requiring concentration and intense mental application. A concert violinist must give up many other pursuits in order to practice the long hours required for achieving his skills. He must even give up some legitimate sports if the practice of these might injure his delicate fingers.

Consider your life and see whether there is an habitual attitude of self-control and inner discipline. Would you say that in all your body, soul and spirit relationships you exercise a mental "alertness" and an inner turning to the indwelling Word of God to put all things in proper proportion? St. Paul exhorted the new Christians of Corinth to bring under captivity and into obedience to Jesus Christ every thought and every imagination *(2 Co 10:5)*.

The end of your Christian life is to love God with your whole heart and all your strength and to love your neighbor as yourself *[Mt 22:37–40]*. But there can be no new level of awareness in prayer that God is our all unless there be a wrenching of ourselves out of the self-containment of a lower level. Asceticism, therefore, is more of a mental attitude that comes through an experience in prayer that God is all-loving. As your learn that He alone must be adored and praised, you manfully strive to put to death all affections and attachments to lesser loves that may become obstacles to your full love of God and neighbor.

TRUE LIBERATION

All too long (and this might explain in your own case why discipline in your spiritual life may have become lessened) we have heard distorted teachings on asceticism. And we were right in rejecting a faulty view of Christianity and human nature. Asceticism for many Christians had become an unhealthy withdrawal from this material world. Through influence from pagan philosophies of Platonism, Manicheanism, Stoicism etc., the early Church through monasticism presented the human body as the source of all evil; therefore it was to be beaten into submission to the spirit.

Appetites that were basically good were held in check by certain practices such as fasting, abstinence, sexual continence etc. The more you "tortured" the body and writhed in pain, the more pleasing you were supposed to be in God's eyes. You were to accept humiliations and always consider yourself the least of all human beings. Is it any wonder that with a more holistic, biblical approach to theology and anthropology, informed by the behavioral sciences such as psychology and sociology, we have justly turned from the old, "traditional" view of asceticism? But have we replaced it with a more informed teaching?

You cannot grow in contemplative prayer nor can you grow into becoming even a successful, loving human being without discipline in all body, soul and spirit relationships. In deep prayer you learn to penetrate within yourself to levels beyond your habitual control, to enter the core of your being and there to find the spark of divine creativity which enables you to give yourself consistently in unselfish love to God and others. This is true liberation, a true expansion of your human consciousness as a person, freely taking your life in hand and giving it back in love to God who has given you all in Christ Jesus. This is a resurrection to a new and higher level of life.

The law of God universally operating on all levels of nature holds true also in regard to your self-development. To "ascend" to a higher form of existence, a greater liberation, you must undergo a "descending" process, a dying to the elements in your total make-up that act as obstacles to a higher mode of existence. The more you live on a purely secular level with no reflective reference to God, the less asceticism will be in your life. The more you give up your selfish aggrandizement by thinking in terms of others in loving service, the more you prepare yourself for a fuller living according to your total nature as God destined you to live.

NEED FOR DISCIPLINE

Today, in our modern pleasure-oriented culture, our bodily appetites are more in need of discipline than ever. But just what forms are to be used will be determined by the goal intended, namely, to love God and neighbor as perfectly as possible. The life of Jesus shows that He had to "go against" His own desires in order to attain His life's goal of doing at all times whatever most pleased His Heavenly Father. The asceticism of Jesus was not separated from His mystical union with the Father. His ascetical practices of going against His own will *(Lk 22:43)* in order to please the Father were always subordinated to the Father and had full meaning insofar as they brought Him into a greater intimate union with His Father.

St. Paul expresses such discipline thus:

"Your mind must be renewed by a spiritual revolution so that you can put on the new self that has been created in God's way, in the goodness and holiness of the truth" *(Ep 4:23-24)*.

In such inner discipline there is always a seemingly negative aspect. Christianity teaches us that there is sin in our members, as St. Paul discovered in his own life *(Rm 7:23)*. Jesus insisted on the inner guarding of the "heart", the deepest level of consciousness within us where motivation for actions is engendered. "But the things that come out of the mouth come from the heart, and it is these that make a man unclean" *(Mt 15:18)*. The vessel had to be cleansed from within and the first step to that cleansing was an inner attentiveness to the thoughts. Jesus knew that where our thoughts are, there will be our treasure *(Lk 12:34)*.

Jesus insisted upon the cross of self-denial in order that you might have a part with Him *(Mt 10:38; 16:24; Mk 8:34; Lk 9:23; 14:27)*. All too often you might think that you would like to follow Jesus Christ, but, like the rich young man in Mark's Gospel, you have too many "possessions" *(Mk 10:17-27)*. There are "enemies", forces both within you and outside of you, attacking you and setting up obstacles against your being your true self as a loving child of God.

St. Peter comes on quite strongly in stressing the need for discipline in the sense of vigilance against the attacks of an enemy:

> "Be sober and watch well; the devil, who is your enemy, goes about roaring like a lion, to find his prey, but you, grounded in the faith, must face him boldly"   *(1 P 5:8)*.

St. Paul describes the spiritual life in terms of a struggle, a battle, a warfare engaged against spiritual forces that seek his destruction. The aim is to seek always the will of God out of loving submission to Him. But this means to enter into the lists, the arena, and stand manfully against the attacks of the evil forces.

> "Draw your strength from the Lord, from the mastery which His power supplies. You must wear all the weapons in God's armor, if you would find strength to resist the cunning of the devil. It is not against flesh and blood that we enter the lists; we have to do with princedoms and powers, with those

who have mastery of the world in these dark days, with malignant influences in an order higher than ours. Take up all God's armor, then, so you will be able to stand your ground when the evil time comes; and be found still on your feet, when all the task is over'' *(Ep 6:10-13)*.

PUTTING ON THE MIND OF CHRIST

Inner discipline is not merely negative. Therapy takes on a positive aspect as it is a means that leads to health. But the spiritual life is more a challenge to embrace full health, the full realization of our spiritual potential, to accept the life that Jesus has come to bring us, that we might have it more abundantly *(Jn 10:10)*. Self-denial, needed to become what you should be in God's eyes, is the therapy that excises your ''false ego'' which holds back your true growth.

In asceticism there is a more positive aspect: that of putting on the mind of Christ, of imitating Him who alone is the way, the truth and the life *(Jn 14:56)*. Putting on the virtues that Jesus lived in His earthly life is, therefore, a necessary part of spiritual discipline that frees you from your sinful self; imitating Him becomes our most powerful motive for living as free children of God. Jesus Himself exhorted His followers: ''Shoulder my yoke and learn from me, for I am gentle and humble in heart and you will find rest for your souls'' *(Mt 11:29-30)*.

His disciples are to turn the other cheek, love all enemies, do good even to those who hurt them. The epistles of the New Testament are nothing but a continued exhortation, not only to avoid sin, but to practice Christ-like virtues. Christianity is a religion of your doing, always presupposing God's grace, in moving your will to desire to live virtuously. This is your *praxis*, your "doing" in order that you may cooperate to live "according to the image and likeness" of God that is Jesus Christ.

But such cooperation again necessitates a control of our appetites which tend toward immoderation. It means imposing limits according to the mind of God communicating the extent of our moderation. And this spells for all of us suffering, a going against ourselves, in a word, the cross that Jesus Christ promised to those who would have a part with Him.

LISTENING TO GOD'S WORD

If God is love, He cannot cease to love you with anything less than an everlasting, perfect love. This means that He is loving you precisely at this moment, in this human encounter with this person, in this moment of sickness, confusion, desire for success, in this situation of humiliation and seeming failure, in that joy and in this cross.

Asceticism for modern Christians must primarily consist in a gentle spirit that listens attentively to God's Spirit revealing that God is now at this moment in-breaking with His infinite love. You practice asceticism and inner discipline when you see that this duty, this action, this passive acceptance of what is being done and cannot be undone, is a part of God's presence. This "place" is holy because God is about to manifest His love and goodness to you in this place.

It will always be beyond you and me to see with our puny minds what is willed by God at every moment in our lives and what God may be permitting to happen. But true discipline in the spiritual life demands of the Christian a faith vision that wants to see God present somehow in each moment and thus to trust and love Him in that moment, to cooperate with His loving activity and in this way seek to glorify Him.

A housewife is being ascetical when she sees that she is praising God more at this moment by preparing food for her hungry family than by going off to a Bible meeting. A student is practicing asceticism when he or she works in the library on a term paper, knowing that it is pleasing to God and part of his or her personal fulfillment at that moment. A child is practicing asceticism when it is time to play and it plays with joy. A husband could please God in no better way than to do his work with energy and joy, honestly and with love for God and family. Thus asceticism looks to the whole person as he or she brings himself or herself in this or that moment under the guiding love of God.

Jacques Leclercq writes of the necessity of bringing all our actions under God:

"In order to unify our life in God, we must direct our thinking, realize what God is, just how all value in general and in particular is related to Him. We shall never set our life in order unless we have clear and habitual consciousness, as actual as possible, of the way in which each of our acts is related to the general task of reduction to the One which we must achieve . . . Action can only be well ordered if we fix our mind in the One to start with. This is achieved in recollection only if our consciousness of the One has become sufficiently deep for us to be able to refer to it spontaneously whenever we are called to act.''

WISDOM, BE ATTENTIVE

If you had ever assisted at the celebration of the Byzantine Liturgy, you would be struck by the many times during the Liturgy that the priest or deacon shouts out to the members of the congregation: ''Wisdom! Be Attentive!'' It is a call to become attentive bodily and in spirit, for Christ, God's Wisdom, is about to come into this community in a new way.

It is this interior activity of one's mind that is all-important in prayer and in the proper use of all creatures to praise God. All external activity, unless the mind or heart accompanies it and directs it to God's praise and glory is useless before God. If your heart, the deepest level of consciousness, is fixed in loving adoration and obedience to God, no enemy can touch you. In fact, then the world of temptations becomes the arena where you, in conflict, can be tested and grow into a deeper, purer love for God.

It is in such temptations that you will discipline yourself to resist the very beginnings of such thoughts. If you allow the temptation to carry you away without going to God, your center, you may set yourself up to accept the suggestion that now has become so attractive to you that you feel you must have it through action. The best resistance to such temptations is to turn within and cry out with St. John Cassian, one of the early Fathers of the desert, ''Oh, Lord, come to my assistance! Oh,

Lord, make haste to help me!" The *Jesus Prayer* is the Eastern Christian's tool to disperse the demonic suggestions by crying out in confidence for the mercy of Jesus: "Lord, Jesus Christ, Son of God, have mercy on me, a sinner!"

NEPSIS

We can learn from the early Fathers of the desert and their teaching about *nepsis*. This word comes from the Greek word, *nepo*, which means to be sober, not inebriated or intoxicated. It refers to a mental sobriety, a mental balance, an internal disposition of attention to the movement of God's Spirit leading you to true discernment of how you should react to a given situation or temptation according to your true dignity as God's loving child. In this state you are not moved impulsively by your own desires or passions, but you hold yourself in abeyance until you know what this or that thought is all about in God's Logos. God is the living criterion of your choices and as often as you choose according to His holy will, the freer you will become as His child. Freedom, therefore, is not primarily having the possibility of choosing good or evil, but ultimately choosing always the good according to God's *Logos*. This is true integration according to the likeness of God, brought about by fidelity to the interior living Word of God within you.

If you allow yourself to go through the day without being inwardly attentive to the presence of God within you, you become progressively more dispersed and more self-centered. The self in you becomes the criterion of your choices, your words and actions. This is the state of *vagueness* described earlier, as a lack of desire to seek God and therefore a movement away from faith in God's hidden presence and the realization that He is the beginning and end of your life.

As you live, so you pray. You can see how important discipline is both in controlling your thoughts and in putting on the mind of Christ. As you positively seek at every moment to bring your will under the dominance of God's holy will, you will truly find that you are praying incessantly as St. Paul exhorts the early Christians to do *(1 Th. 5:18)*.

SOME PRINCIPLES

In a teaching prepared for *Crux* entitled: *Following Jesus in the Real World: Asceticism Today,* I brought together some principles that may be helpful for you as you seek to bring discipline into your spiritual life.

1. The first principle is that any and all ascetical practices must always be considered as means to attain the end of the full perfection of the spiritual life. The value of any practice derives from the interior motivation to aid one's growth in the spiritual life, through therapeutic correctives to offset the influences of sin in all its self-centeredness, and in the positive development of Christ-like virtues.

2. The whole person must be the subject of continual discipline. We must see individual acts of self-control in their role played in the whole picture of the spiritual life. You cannot focus your attention and curb only your bodily appetites while giving free rein to your inner imagination. You are

a whole person, made up of body, soul and spirit relationships.

3. There must be a hierarchy in your ascetical practices. Certain areas of your being are more important in determining your choices than others. You have to place more importance upon some ascetical practices than others, without neglecting any area of your being. The interior faculties of memory, understanding and will require a more constant control since it is through these faculties that your moral decisions are made to sin or to practice virtuous deeds.

4. All ascetical practices, especially those of "mortification" or control over the bodily appetites, should be practiced with prudence and discretion. Every person is different and has different needs, having received different gifts of grace. Prudence dictates that whatever practices are used, your must always be able adequately to perform your duties of life.

AREAS OF DISCIPLINE

If you are to grow in deeper prayer and oneness with God, striving at every moment to seek to please Him, you must concretely zero in upon the various areas that make up your life.

1. *Discipline of the body and exterior senses.* There are many hindrances to success in prayer, such as preoccupation with work, bad health, sluggishness and sleepiness in the morning etc., but these eventually are overcome and do not bar real success. But lack of consistent discipline in the control of the body and the exterior senses will always bring about a state of dissipation and self-centeredness which destroys any true, self-

surrendering prayer. Here we might examine our indulgence in the matter of food, drink, sleep, sex, smoking. Does fasting have any place in your life? The indiscriminate watching of TV without discipline can destroy any desire to pray. Do you watch TV excessively? What type of program do you watch? How many hours a day do you give to watching TV?

2. *Discipline of the Inner Senses.* You are not to ignore or allow to atrophy your faculties of imagination and memory. Yet these gifts must be under discipline and control of right reason and a grace-filled will. To avoid dissipation, strive to expel from the very first moment of awareness any fancies and reveries that seem either to be a dangerous occasion for sin or merely to be worthless. Idle daydreaming, useless musings and fancies not only waste a great deal of time, but pave the way to more thoughts of self-absorption. Seek to do with energy and attention all that you are doing at the given moment, doing it for God's glory. Feed your imagination and direct the memory with wholesome thoughts from Scripture and the Liturgy, from spiritual books and the beauties of nature.

3. *Control of the Emotions.* There never was a saint who did not become one by the help of his or her strong passions, brought under the dominance of grace informing the intellect and will. Your "concupiscible" and "irascible" appetites are powerful for good or evil depending on how you control them and direct them according to the mind of God. When you are led by blind passions, union with God cannot be attained, for a greater force propels you away from being God-centered.

4. *Discipline of the Intellect*. It is your intellect that enlightens the will as to what to do as good and what to avoid as evil. Under the name of *conscience*, it is the guide for your moral life. All of us have need to discipline how we use our intellects, what we allow to enter into our minds from our reading and curious thinking. Often we need discipline in the positive manner of developing our intellect by ways of disciplined study.

5. *Asceticism of the Will*. It is here that you make your choices for good or evil. Discipline is needed to avoid a lack of reflection, over-eagerness, fretting, worry etc. Sloth and fear of failure can cripple the proper use of your will. Basically, self-love in the will is at the root of all movement away from God.

These inner disciplines, when constantly practiced, enable you to become "seed." Seed must remain in the ground to die, bear fruit and give its yield to others. The immersion of this "seed" into the deep, still waters of a disciplined life in prayer feeds, nurtures and produces a fusion of the soul into God. From this comes a "bursting forth" into vibrant life, a putting away of the old and taking on the new. It is your whole person constantly evolving into a closer assimilation to the image and likeness of God.

5

Fasting

It is the Church's call to all of us to be led by the Holy Spirit as Jesus was into the desert, but in place of the literal desert, you and I are called to enter into the desert of our hearts. When you turn within and descend into your deeper self, beyond the habitual pre-conditioning of your sensual, emotional and intellectual baggage, you hear the voice calling you to a change of heart, a conversion, *a metanoia*.

The desert is not the end of your wanderings. You are heading through the experience in the inner desert toward the Promised Land to greater oneness in loving union with the indwelling Trinity and with your neighbor. One means known throughout the life of Jesus, His first disciples and down through the ages among all of His more ardent, faithful followers to reach the inner "still point" of complete listening and total self-surrender to the direction of God's Holy Spirit has always been the practice of *fasting*.

Has fasting been a habitual exercise of yours in your following of Christ, to help you become more focused upon God's indwelling Word, Jesus Christ? Have you experienced the "laying down your life" for your brothers and sisters suffering throughout the world through experiencing the "crunch" of physical pains by giving up food out of love for them? Has fasting given you the cleansing effects on the physical, psychical and spiritual levels that the Spirit wishes to give you as you stretch out toward the Heavenly Jerusalem?

Many of you wish to know how to go about the art of fasting. I offer this chapter on fasting to encourage you to make this practice a habitual one in your spiritual life. You will be amazed at the results in your prayer-life and even in your physical health. But more importantly you will experience how to do what Yahweh is asking of you: " . . . only this, to act justly, to love tenderly and to walk humbly with your God" *(Mi 6:8)*.

Once the disciples of Jesus were asked by the father of an epileptic boy to heal him, but they were unable to do so. Jesus healed the boy and when the disciples asked Him privately: "Why were we unable to cast it out?" Jesus answered: "This is the kind that can only be driven out by prayer and fasting," *(Mk 9:29)*. Has not prayer, reinforced by fasting, disappeared by and large from your spiritual life?

When was the last time you seriously fasted? When was the last time you went 24 hours without some solid food to eat? What sort of fasting, both physical (abstinence from solid food) and spiritual (going against your selfishness by doing good to those in need) did you perform last year during Lent? Is Lent any special time different from other times in your year, a time to fast, weep and mourn for your sins and rend your heart in a true conversion back to the Lord?

Why has fasting become a lost art for so many Christians? For Catholics, the fast and abstinence laws of the Church have been radically changed in the past decades. When Pope Pius XII, on January 6, 1953, changed the eucharistic fast from midnight until Communion time, a practice observed since the fourth century, he cited the social and economic changes of modern society. Pope Paul VI on February 19, 1966, completely modified the fast and abstinence regulations, allowing Catholics to eat meat on Friday and holding to a compulsory fast during Lent only on Ash Wednesday and Good Friday.

Many of us see the greater importance, as Pope Paul VI insisted, of spiritual works of charity and the faithful fulfillment of our daily duties; but in the process of doing away with a church discipline which was uniform for all, we effectively lost also the practice of fasting. Another reason why fasting has not had a regular place of importance in our spiritual lives is the worldly materialism that has made its inroads into our own spiritual life. We naturally tend to avoid any physical suffering. The more physical comforts we enjoy, the more they become necessary, so we think.

Another reason is that, before the charismatic renewal in the Church, there had not been a greatly developed sensitivity to the Holy Spirit in our lives, with a deep lively faith in the Word of God from Holy Scripture. To fast in a personalized Christian way, one needs to consult the Holy Spirit constantly.

At present there is a return to fasting. This has

come to some through proper dieting. Others have returned to Scripture and the writings of the great Saints to discover anew the constant teaching and practice of fasting as an integral part of serious religious life in Christ. Contact with the Far Eastern disciplines like Hinduism, Yoga, Zen Buddhism and mind-expanding techniques has stirred yet others to return to fasting.

For some of us, as we view the poverty, physical hunger and starvation of millions throughout the world, especially in the sub-Sahara and Ethiopia, fasting has become a need to "suffer" with those suffering. Lanza del Vasto, one of Gandhi's disciples, once wrote: "When you think of men starving in the world you are forced to cry out for them with a more sensitive heart. One who fasts is made transparent. Others appear to him transparent. Their sufferings enter into him and he is without defense against them."

How can you and I continue to eat three square meals a day, continue to be overweight and dispose of quantities of food as garbage when we see the hungry and starving throughout the world? But above all, how can we face Christ and consider ourselves His disciples if we do not return to fasting? A change is taking place among many people in regard to fasting. They are discovering that it has been shown scientifically that eating less red meat, more vegetables and fruits, with occasional purification of our digestive system, through fasting, is a tremendous help toward bodily health.

How much more important to you is fasting if you are to lead a deeper spiritual life? As you strip yourself of all pseudo-sophistication and return, as the Gospel enjoins, to become like a little child in order to enter into the Kingdom of Heaven, i.e. into the basic relationships with the Almighty, Transcendent Being, God, you find yourself returning to fasting as a religious act necessary for a healthy total existence.

Primitive man was aware of the ethical strength that could bolster the moral fiber of an individual or a community when he restrained his basic appetite for food by periodic fasting. Man, universally throughout all cultures and civilizations, feels the need to fast in order to offer to God penance and propitiation for sins. Carl Jung speaks to the modern world of the universal need of all of us in society to establish a *rite de sortie*, a way of providing a religious catharsis and thus a return of man and society once again to a new relationship with the Absolute.

Religious fasting is an intentional abstention from food out of religious motives. It is essentially an act of the higher nature of ourselves, a prelude to a higher life of the spirit wherein we make contact with the Unapproachable God. When you and I fail to control the amount of food we eat and freely indulge without any moderation, this disturbs the inner order of the spirit of dependence upon the Almighty.

CHRISTIAN FASTING

But we are speaking here of Christian fasting. And it must be the Holy Spirit who leads you further into the Christian values of fasting, deeper than those which were evident to primitive man. Many speak of "spiritual fasting," which refers to abstinence from sins or vices. This type of fasting

67

is absolutely necessary for Christian salvation. We find in all of us areas of pride, selfishness, a will to control others' lives and events, concupiscence, etc. from which we must "fast."

But Holy Scripture (as well as our own personal experience) shows us that there will be little control or moderation in our personal lives unless there is also something of violence—a dying process. "From John the Baptizer's time until now the kingdom of God has suffered violence, and the violent take it by force" (Mt 11:12).

St. Paul exhorts us to control our lust for food and not make an idol of it, as some of the Israelites did in the desert (1 Co 10:7). "What I do is discipline my own body and master it, for fear that after having preached to others I myself should be rejected" (1 Co 9:27). St. Paul and the other early Christians had inherited an understanding of the importance of fasting from the Old Testament.

The word usually used in the Old Testament is *tsoum*, referring generally to a voluntary privation of food, especially for a religious purpose. It often included an appeal to sorrow for sins and a penitential propitiation (eg. Is 58:3-7; Ez 9:1-15). Often it has the sense of creating an experience of one's creatureliness, his interior poverty and alienation from the All-Holy because of sinfulness.

Individuals in the Old Testament, such as Moses, Elias, Daniel and David, fasted for various reasons. Usually the element of expiation is present in Old Testament fasting. The accent on a physical fast kept both the corporal suffering, through abstaining from nourishment, and the interior sorrow and conversion of heart together in the Hebraic world. The prophet Joel well summarized this double purpose of fasting when he called his people to a fast and repentance through God's message given to him. "Return to me with your whole heart, with fasting, and weeping and mourning" *(Jl 2:12).*

Both in the Old and New Testaments fasting always was meant to be a total experience that began with the total "bodied" being suffering vitally his/her own nothingness as he/she stood before God to beg for forgiveness. To fast is to be afflicted, humbled to adopt the conduct and comportment which becomes a sinful creature.

THE TEACHING OF JESUS ON FASTING

Jesus came to fulfill the Old Covenant. The same elements, inspired by the same Holy Spirit working within God's chosen people, as found in the Old Testament fasting were to continue in Christian fasting. Fasting was to be an appeal to sorrow for sins along with a propitiation for sins committed. It was an exercise of imploration to obtain God's mercy and protection.

When Jesus began to teach about Christian fasting, He sought to correct the hypocrisy of the Pharisees who fasted externally without a true inner conversion of heart. Yet He wanted to give fasting a whole new dimension that it had not possessed in the Old Testament. There were to be no long faces during a fast; but joy would be the quality that would accompany the Christian fast.

"When you fast do not put on a gloomy look as the hypocrites do: they pull long faces to let men know they are fasting. I tell you solemnly, they have had their reward. But when you fast, put oil on your head and wash your face, so that no one will know you are fasting except your Father who sees all that is done in secret; and your Father who sees all that is done in secret will reward you" *(Mt 6:16-18)*.

The joyful element that Jesus adds as a necessary ingredient to fasting does not take away from the suffering and dying process that is essential to a fast. But the Christian belief that Jesus "is risen and has trampled down death, granting death to those in the tomb" (Prayer from the Byzantine Easter Liturgy) fills the Christian who fasts with an experience of exultation and triumph even amidst the suffering and bite of a partial death, symbolized by fasting. Fasting leads to the spirit-surrender of self to God that gives the joy of the Holy Spirit *(Ga 5:22)*

Fasting in the life of Jesus is an experiential living out of the eschatological hope central in the paschal mystery. While Christ was on earth, He was the Bridegroom. He had come to establish the mystical marriage with God's People. How could His disciples fast and suffer during such a celebration of joy? *(Mt 9:14-15)*. The good news was at hand. The Kingdom of God was indeed close in the very person of Jesus Christ!

But after Jesus died and rose, His followers, including you and me, are found in a period of awaiting His full coming. "While we are in the body, we are absent from the Lord," says St. Paul *(2 Co 5:6)*. We wait in suffering, longing for the Bridegroom to return in all His beauty and glory. Yet this exile of suffering shows to the world a hopeful joy. This joy results from knowing that even now Jesus Christ has conquered in such a fasting experience the possession of our whole being. Even now we are "new creatures" raised to sonship and daughtership with Him, co-heirs forever of Heaven. Death can have no sting for us. This is what we Christians announce to the despondent world. The suffering of this life, of this fasting, cannot be compared to the joys to come! Yet even now as we die in such suffering, we experience greater, unending, joyful union with the Lamb of God!

FASTING—AN ACT OF LOVE

Once you, through your fasting, have broken your independent hold over your life and surrendered yourself totally into the loving hands of God, you find a fresh openness in loving service toward others. You empathize in a new consciousness with all the physical, psychical and spiritual needs of every human being. Walls of division and prejudice fall as you run to meet the crying needs of your neighbor. You understand that you cannot take on all of the sufferings of the whole universe, of every broken man, woman and child.

Yet fasting will give you a sense of your own poverty and creatureliness. You are also the poorest of all God's children. When you learn of others suffering from a lack of food, clothing, housing, you cannot indulge any longer in any form of excess. You become a prophet not only in word, but in deed. Here you see how actual, physical fasting develops the necessary spiritual fasting: controlled moderation in every area of sensual, emotional and intellectual life so that all

71

sinful thoughts, words and deeds are eliminated and universal charity reigns supreme in your life. God has conquered in your life and this is proved by your love for others.

You may not be called by God to do penance for the immoderations of injustice to others; you may not be called to be a "punishment" to the conscience of the guilty as Mahatma Gandhi felt called to be. But for some modern Christians a fast could be public, demonstrated for all to see, a dramatic protest against excessive nuclear armament or racial discrimination on the social or religious levels. There is a grave responsibility for such prophetic "fasters" to move at each step in humble prayer under the power and guidance of the Holy Spirit.

HOW TO FAST

There are all sorts of forms that fasting can take. We can speak of abstinence from meat or other foods while still taking solid nourishment in other forms. A fast, however, implies giving up any solid nourishment. A partial fast consists in taking no nourishment except liquids such as juices, milk, broths, etc. This is an excellent form of fasting to begin with.

The *normal* fast is to take only water. Water is most important to flush the system, since it burns up the waste material found in the digestive tract as well as the stored-up fats and sugars. One should drink as much water as one wishes. A beginner in fasting should first give up one meal. Then some days later, drop two meals. Then a few days later, try a whole day with nothing but water. Gradually the fast can be increased to two or three consecutive days.

Another way of beginning to move into a normal fast with only water is to increase the fast to five or seven days, taking liquids such as orange juice, soup, broth, etc. I have found it a very effective fast of a week or ten days to take only warm milk with honey and a bit of dissolved peanut butter for protein. One can continue to do normal work without any loss of energy or efficiency; on the contrary, one will usually experience a surge of creative energy!

The length of the fast and the manner or style will depend on our situation in life, work-load etc. Discernment of the Holy Spirit is necessary, especially to determine the length. An effective fast is one of from three to five days, with water and dissolved honey with a few drops of lemon.

BREAKING THE FAST

Most people who have fasted for any length of time will agree that there is usually no danger in fasting itself, up to 25 days of fast. One who is diabetic or hypoglycemic should normally not go on a strict water fast. But the real question is how to come off the fast. One should usually begin to return to normal eating habits by first taking a liquid diet of fresh juices, milk, cream of wheat cereal etc. Then light foods such as yogurt, thin soups and cottage cheese, which prepares one for more solid food such as bread, cheese, eggs and lastly meat if desired. One must be cautious in that after an extended fast hunger will take over as one begins to eat food, even light food. Eating too much too fast can lead to edema, digestive upset and general disorder.

After a longer fast, the lost weight is restored quite readily; at least one returns to what should be his/her "normal weight." Fasting does bring us to that optimal weight level, and it is imperative that one thereafter maintain that weight or he/she will lose the values attained in the fast. This applies not only to the physical, but to the spiritual values as well.

During any extended fast, you should devote the time that normally would have been spent in eating at table to more time with the Lord in prayer and spiritual reading. A Christian fast is always a spiritual work as well as a physical undertaking. It is the whole person seeking to open him/herself to the operations of God. Throughout the Bible, God has clearly encouraged us to fast as one of the best means to enter into purity of heart. Fasting will always be a vital means of growing into the integrated person we must be to live fully unto the Lord. You will soon find that fasting will be an important part of your prayer-life; namely, that no deep prayer-life can develop without some form of inner and physical moderation that allows you to stand vigilant over your own selfish desires and to yield to God's love.

God is calling us on our journey, to a daily practice of self-denial. This journey is a walk in faith to freedom, a freedom won through the mastery of body, mind and spirit. Your answer to this call from your Lord and Master leads you through the desert into loving submission to the Logos living within you. Your steps become hurried as you breathe in your new oneness with the Word made flesh. You move forward feeling truly alive, for your dying to self in humility and repentance has brought you forth in new resurrection.

6

Spiritual Experiences in Prayer

God is everywhere, so close. All you have to do is stretch out and touch Him in all of His creatures and in His wonderful creation! He is always meeting you in new and exciting ways. And you, with child-like faith, open your eyes with wonder and expectancy to meet Him in the swiftness of each moment as it descends upon you to sweep you up into His eternal embrace.

Such intimacy, when God seemingly bends down to your littleness and lifts you suddenly into His immediate embrace, occurs from time to time with varying intensity and with varying responses on your part. Sometimes these moments of intimacy give you encouragement and consolation to continue the pilgrimage through the dry desert. At other times such touches by God give you a call and a direction which you have been seeking in conformity with His holy will. Many times we are confused at the psychic manifestations that accompany God's presence. What is real and what is illusion?

As you grow in deeper prayer, you enter into an

increasing surrender of yourself to the activity of God in your prayer. The tendency is to move away from your conscious control in prayer to an opening of yourself to God by entering the innermost core of your being. Here great discipline is required, for amazing and frightening things can happen.

As you pass through layers of psychic experiences to reach that inner "still point" where God speaks to you in the cloud of unknowing, psychic powers can be released. Repressed material that has been buried in the unconscious can rise up threateningly to disturb you in prayer. Erotic feelings can influence your entire body. Flashes and lights, psychic powers of telepathy can come forth. Visions and locutions or voices can occur, temperature changes can come over your entire body. Shaking of certain bodily parts can occur. At times these experiences can bring you a wonderful sense of peace and contentment. At other times, such experiences can be filled with fearful images and threatening voices, as darkness belches over your entire psychic apparatus, leaving you in desolation and almost despair as to God's presence and His love for you.

In all of these spiritual experiences, what is reality? What comes from God and what is hallucination in the beckoning visions of enticing forms that whirl over the screen of your consciousness? Visions, voices, levitational experiences, out-of-the-body experiences, touches, celestial odors can be intensely experienced. What are the meanings of such spiritual experiences? Before we discuss the meaning of these experiences, let us clearly distinguish the various kinds of experiences in deeper prayer—or even at the very beginning of the spiritual life—dealt with by spiritual writers.

TYPES OF SPIRITUAL EXPERIENCES

Dr. Gerald May, in his highly recommended book, *Care of Mind; Care of Spirit* distinguishes two general experiences: 1. spiritual experiences of union; and 2. experiences in which the self-image is preserved. In the first type of experience, all activities such as thinking, imagining, emoting that serve to define oneself become suspended, yet awareness remains open, clear and vibrant. Perhaps you had a sudden, spontaneous experience, whether religious or not, that allowed you to sense your complete oneness with someone or some creature of nature. The "yourself" seemingly disappears. You are not in the power seat directing reality but reality engulfs you so powerfully and suddenly that you only sense a global oneness with all around you. This is what the classic writers of the mystical life call "infused contemplation." Its essence can be described as all self-definition becoming suspended while your awareness remains clear and wide open, excluding nothing.

The other general category of spiritual experiences stresses the preservation of the self-image. You are a free, positing agent, quite in charge experiencing something happening to you, of which you are fully aware. This category embraces all so-called non-unitive experiences, which comprise the majority of spiritual experiences.

Such experiences occurring in prayer can be of three main kinds: *1) Sensory experiences* that range from activating one's imagination, as St. Ignatius in his *Spiritual Exercises* encourages the retreatant to "contemplate" Christ in the Gospel scenes as though the retreatant were sensibly present to the scenes contemplated, to spontaneous inner visions, the hearing of internal voices, the seeing of light and the feeling of hot flashes throughout the body; *2) Intellectual insights* that partake of an inner "vision" without any sensible image involved; *3) Extrasensory experiences* of a parapsychological nature such as out-of-the-body experiences, precognition, telepathy, seeing auras around others and even telekinetic experiences.

Not all spiritual experiences in prayer are consoling and pleasant and confirming. As you open deeper levels of the unconscious to the presence of God, the hidden areas of what can be called the "demonic" forces from within and from without, can present themselves to you in a fierce, attacking way. I have dealt with this problem in a published teaching on the occult that deals with obsession and possession and the seemingly schizophrenic condition that results from entering into deeper levels of prayer

ATTITUDE TOWARD SUCH EXPERIENCES

The great Christian mystics over the centuries have been unanimous in stressing humility and compunction as the true touchstones of a religious experience that is begun in God and completed in Him for His glory. St. John of the Cross gives us very sound advice in this matter:

"And it must be known that although all these things may happen to the bodily senses in the way of God, we must never rely upon them or accept them, but must fly from them, without trying to ascertain whether they be good or evil; for, the more completely exterior and corporeal they are, the less certainly they are of God . . . So he that esteems such things errs greatly and exposes himself to great peril of being deceived; in any case he will have within himself a complete impediment to the attainment of spirituality.''

There has been a universal caution also among the Eastern Fathers from St. Ephrem to St. Gregory Palamas of the 14th Century in regard to any extraordinary psychic phenomena that have repercussions especially on the sense levels. The basic reason is that such spiritual experiences can be so satisfying to the false ego in all human beings that our self-centered drive for power and control, even over God, soon seeks such phenomena to build up a greater sense of illusion and separation from God. Pride can so easily convince us that we are becoming holy by enjoying experiences that all great saints also enjoyed.

Still we do believe that God wishes to give Himself to us directly through an immediate experience. His love is so overwhelming that He strives to draw us into the union of His triune life. Such communication and self-giving on the part of God is made to a human person, a whole being, an ''embodied'' being, calling that person not to be a separated soul or a detached intellect. As you begin your spiritual journey inward to meet God as the Ground of your being, God does flood you with graces of His felt presence. Such sensible consolations give you strength and help in the building up of interior faith in God's presence as love so that you can surrender more and more to meeting Him in the darkness of even purer faith.

Spiritual discernment is necessary in such spiritual experiences to see whether they really are helping to lead you to greater union with God through faith, hope and love, or whether they are obstacles to that union. Psychologists are also interested in such phenomena, but more so because of the content experienced, while spiritual direction is concerned not only with what has been experienced in prayer, but above all the manner in which the individual receives the experience and responds to it.

Dr. May gives us an important distinction so that we may avoid a simplistic and erroneous dualism that separates the workings of the Holy Spirit from the inner psychic dynamism which must necessarily be the stage on which we human individuals are to experience God calling us to greater oneness with Him in prayer.

"Too much emphasis on self-vs.- God encourages an artificial and erroneous dualism, rashly separating one's inner psychological experience from the workings of the Holy Spirit in our lives. The fact is, of course, that God often speaks to us and works in us through our psychological experience. Mediated and altered as they may be by our personal attachments and preconceptions, the manifestations of grace are as truly present in our subjective psychology as in a sunset or a rainbow. Further, preoccupation with considerations of psyche-vs.- God can lead, paradoxically, to an unintended preoccupation with the psyche itself. The human mind presents so much material to deal with that it can easily become a quagmire for the curious. Thus to invest oneself in separating psychodynamics from the revelations of God can become a distortion not unlike excessive spiritual warfare; it can become as much of a distraction as seeking God solely *through* psychology. Both extremes occur all too frequently in modern spiritual guidance because of our society's ambivalent obsession with psychology."

VISIONS

Today, especially through an increased interest in prayer and through the charismatic renewal, the subject of visions is one of interest and also concern. When a person in a prayerful group witnesses in great detail to a vision that he or she received from the Lord, what sort of discernment should be given to such an experience? You perhaps have entered into a "presence" of God that was very real and intimate but without any sensible form. Was God presenting Himself to you in a real way or was this merely your own imagination?

The Catholic Church has had a long tradition of solid teaching on this subject. Teachers such as St. Teresa of Avila and St. John of the Cross teach us an acceptable doctrine on visions. They distinguish visions as corporeal, imaginative or intellectual.

Corporeal visions involve a sense form that seemingly originates outside of the one "seeing" it. Without passing judgment on their veracity, the visions of St. Bernadette of Lourdes and the three children of Fatima would be of this class.

In this type of vision, one must exercise great

caution since such a sense vision can be of an hallucinatory nature. Teachers of tried virtue and wisdom warn us to flee from such a type of vision as well as sense locutions or sense experiences that appeal directly to the sense of smell, touch or taste. In the words of St. John of the Cross:

" . . . a person must not fix the eyes of his soul upon the figure and object supernaturally according to him, whether the object pertains to the exterior senses (locutions and words to the sense of hearing; visions of saints and beautifully resplendent lights to the sense of sight; fragrance to the sense of smell; delightful tastes to the other pleasures derived from the palate; and to the sense of touch . . . .) or whether it is an interior imaginative vision. He must instead renounce them all."

The second type of vision is that of an imaginative kind. These are formed in one's imagination or outside. If the imagination is actively involved in furnishing the images, there is the great danger of self-delusion. There are two other types of imaginative visions: 1) Either the images take place within our imagination but the images arise from nothing that we have previously experienced through our senses; or, 2) God gives us a vision not furnished by our imagination that seemingly takes place outside of ourselves. An example of an imaginative vision taking place within our imagination but with images not furnished by previous sense experiences would be a vision of Heaven with God in His glory. To see a vision outside of ourselves in the imagination without the imagination furnishing the images would be to see the saints with their glorified, spiritualized bodies.

The type of vision where God operates most directly is the intellectual vision that takes place in the human understanding without any medium of sense images. Here there is the least possibility of your own selfish projection or the operations of the demonic upon you. God gives you an experiential knowledge which He imprints directly upon you of a truth that He wishes to reveal to you. In this sense you can come from prayer, "seeing" a truth more clearly than ever before in your entire life and yet be unable to describe in images how you arrived at such new knowledge. Your life is changed by this vision. Perhaps, for example, you could receive a new intellectual vision of how Jesus is totally present in the Eucharist, without division, in His entire humanity and divinity, and that He continues always to extend that eucharistic presence to you at all times. This powerful knowledge is an experience that could change your life.

VOICES

Voices or locutions are words that are spoken to you in prayer. Again we distinguish various levels. Words come to you as though they are spoken to you sensibly outside of yourself. These are very susceptible to delusion, as they are so rooted in your senses. But the more interior and intellectual these words are, heard from within, the less they can lead you astray and the more God can operate to reveal to you words of wisdom, knowledge and understanding. Such interior words partake of a prophetic role and can serve to strengthen and encourage you to reveal hidden mysteries to be taught to others, or to rebuke you or others.

The distinctive characteristics of God's interior words spoken to you in prayer are that such words are useful (to a holy purpose) and there is a precise clarity. You should normally hold yourself in inner attention and detachment as your surrender yourself to God's leading. Then if such words are an illusion of the imagination or a suggestion from the devil, they will disappear or at least do you little harm. If, however, they are from God, the effects will be seen at once. St. John of the Cross gives us excellent advice that we should apply to all psychic phenomena of any kind:

> "If such experience be of God, it produces its effect upon the spirit at the very moment when it appears or is felt, without giving the soul time or opportunity to deliberate whether it will accept or reject it. For, even as God gives these things supernaturally, without effort on the part of the soul, and independent of its capacity, God produces in it the effect that He desires by means of such things; . . . it is as if fire were applied to a person's naked body; it would matter little whether or not he wished to be burned; the fire would of necessity accomplish its work."

TEARS

In the area, however, of the gift of tears we find in the writings of the mystics, especially of the Christian East, an encouragement that, rather than be guarded, we should pray for this external manifestation. The gift of tears can happen so often and so readily and its supernatural source can be easily discerned. It admits of much intensity and duration that may vary from a few tears shed now and then in prayer, to a state that may last through several years of uninterrupted weeping.

For most Americans, weeping is often associated with weakness and emotionalism. But the common consensus of the good that such tears can produce in prayer when they flow as a gift from God, was taught unanimously both among the Eastern and Western Fathers. Tears were seen by such Fathers as a sign that the mind in prayer was leaving the prison of this world and entering into a new age.

Tears that are a gift from God have the power and action to destroy and uproot sin and passion and any obstacle preventing a person from letting God have His full way in one's life. Tears illumine the dark recesses of the soul to bring it under the light of Christ's teaching and powerful healing. Peace and joy result from experiencing the love of God toward a sinful individual.

The true test of the value of tears must not be found in the quantity of tears shed but in the brokenness of spirit experienced before the awesome majesty of God who is so tender, so loving and such a healing Father.

GUIDELINES

We can summarize what has already been said about spiritual experiences occurring in prayer by the following principles and guidelines.

1. Be cautious not to attribute every action in prayer to the direct intervention of the Holy Spirit

(See teaching on how to evaluate the charismatic experience of being slain in the Spirit). This is especially important, as it has already been pointed out in this teaching, in the cases of phenomena that are rooted in the senses of seeing, hearing, touching, tasting or smelling. This does not deny that God could give you such a sense of His presence in such an experience. But we see many persons in mental hospitals or those using transcendental methods of meditation on a merely natural plane who receive such experiences with very little transcendent change in their lives. By their fruits shall you know them.

2. Such experiences are never to be sought for in prayer. It is a great temptation to want such phenomena for the psychic satisfaction they bring to us. In no way should these experiences be construed as a measure of your advance in sanctity. The true test of greater growth in sanctity must be measured by your growth in forgetting your own selfish interests and living in loving service toward others, God and neighbor.

3. If such experiences happen with any frequency, consult a Spirit-filled and experienced spiritual director who can lead you to an indifference toward receiving such phenomena and guide you to a true discernment as to their real source, and your line of conduct and response toward them.

4. The true test of authentic prayer can never be measured by psychic phenomena and how many "spiritual experiences" one has had, but by one's surrendering love and submission to God's will. If you are touching God, with or without any psychic phenomena accompanying your prayer, this will be measured by the true thermometer of

increasing love of God and humble service toward your neighbor, especially the ones that are closest to you in your family.

5. In experiencing erotic feelings in prayer, especially when you are praying to the human Christ, seek to rise beyond the erotic effects and desires. Do not entertain thoughts or take up positions in prayer or do any actions that would intensify such feelings. You need not give up praying to the human Christ, but greater humility and purity of heart are called for.

6. In cases of ecstasies, raptures or out-of-the-body experiences, the test of divine origin is what you may learn in such a state, which should lead you to greater charity and humility. If these experiences truly come from God, you will know it from the effects produced. You will be overwhelmed by the greatness of God and your own nothingness. This knowledge will fill you with peace and joy, a new detachment from everything created, and a firm adhesion to seek always to please God. Such spiritual effects will separate the true gift of God in authentic ecstasy, rapture or out-of-the-body experiences from those induced by physical collapse, hallucination or autosuggestion.

ABANDONMENT

Prayer is truly a pilgrimage that moves gradually away from your own control over God through your words and images and affections that you conjure up in prayer to an ever-increasing abandonment to God's immediate self-giving to you as He wishes and when He wishes. He becomes the free God that you allow to have total dominion over every facet of your life.

These are some of the problem areas that persons interested in prayer may encounter along their journey into that mysterious union between themselves and God. Not all problems could be touched upon; above all, not all treated adequately. The closer you move toward the BURNING BUSH, the more rules no longer can be an adequate guide. They serve only as sign posts that it is hoped will allow you to run courageously in the ways of the Lord. True prayer is ultimately love.

To the degree that you surrender yourself freely to the leadership of the indwelling Trinity in each moment, to that degree can you consider yourself as a person of authentic prayer and a true Christian. You will be led from moment to moment into greater light, as you see God's loving presence in all events by increased faith, hope and love. Complete abandonment is the Holy Spirit's gift to you if you are ready to die to your false self and begin to live in the truth of the new creature that you are and have always been in the eyes of the Heavenly Father who eternally loves you in Jesus Christ through His Spirit.

A fitting conclusion to this chapter on prayer are the words of Hugh of St. Victor:

"Yes, it is truly the Beloved who visits you. But he comes—invisible, hidden, incomprehensible. He comes to touch you, not to be seen; to intimate His presence to you, not to be understood; to make you taste of Him, not to pour Himself out in His entirety; to draw your affection, not to satisfy your desire;

to bestow the first-fruits of His love, not to communicate it in its fullness.

Behold in this the most certain pledge of your future marriage: that you are destined to see Him to possess Him eternally, because He already gives Himself to you at times to taste; with what sweetness you know.

Therefore, in the times of His absence you shall console yourself; and during His visits you shall renew your courage which is ever in need of heartening. We have spoken at great length, O my soul, I ask you to think of none but Him, listen to none but Him, to take hold of none but Him, possess none but him."

7

Seeking Spiritual Direction-a "Soul Friend"

What you and I are desperately in need of is guidance in forming our Christian life in Christ. We no longer live in a Christian society or culture. In fact, consumerism tends to exalt the individual and his or her basic sense appetites. Our senses are being constantly bombarded by enticing attractions that hypnotically fill us with a restless desire to possess them.

Christians are to be a leaven in the dough of humanity, a transforming power of love and enlightenment in a selfish, dark world. But concretely, where do you go to receive your power to love and to be enlightened? This is the constant plea that I hear in traveling around the country: "Where can I find a prayerful community in which I can grow in the Lord? Where can I find spiritual direction that will guide me in my Christian life? Is spiritual direction really necessary?"

I would like to look at this topic of seeking spiritual direction from a guide, learned in the laws of the spiritual life and experienced personally in holiness and submission to the inner movements of the Spirit.

At times such a guide can help us on an occasional basis in a retreat, through a meeting, a written article or book or a tape. At other times such a "soul-friend" will offer his/her loving guidance over a longer period of regular meetings. To find such a friend in the Spirit is a great grace. Yet even in such a spiritual direction situation, the last word must be given to the main director in the spiritual life, and that is the Holy Spirit.

Everywhere I go in the United States and Canada I hear the universal complaint: "But where can I find a good spiritual director?" Persons eager to go deeper into prayer and make continued progress in the spiritual life and in following the leadings of the Holy Spirit know that they have need of discernment other than their own insights or opinions. You can be so easily duped into thinking that God thinks as you think, that your judgments about yourself and others and even God are really objectively true. How can you be sure that you are truly listening to God's Word and following his commands in docile obedience?

The difficulties that travelers encounter along the spiritual way are so great and each of us knows that the ignorance within us is so vast and insidious that we all have need of having some kind of a guide. Thomas Merton writes:

"The most dangerous man in the world is the contemplative who is guided by nobody. He trusts his own visions. He obeys the attractions of an interior voice but will not listen to other men."

St. Teresa of Avila advises the traveler "to consult some learned person if he can, and the more learned the person the better. Those who walk in the way of prayer have the greater need of learning; and the more spiritual they are, the greater is their need . . ."

NEED FOR A SPIRITUAL DIRECTOR

Besides the many psychological dangers that lurk along the path of those who enter the interior castle, there are other perils. The traveler may be bewitched by the beauty he or she encounters: delightful experiences, voices, visions, beautiful thoughts about God, or just the restful peace that fills one's being. All these can become snares if a person clings to them. One must push on, clinging absolutely to nothing created, in order to be attentive to the living flame of love that tenderly wounds the soul at its deepest center.

You need spiritual direction just to begin the spiritual journey. Without it, there is usually no beginning at all. You will begin to travel unsteadily, unsurely, and often weighed down by many false principles. It is similar to taking off in an airplane. Once off the ground all is well. Once the Spirit takes us on wing, all is well. But help is needed in the beginning. Just as the airplane pilot is in need of specific knowledge applied to his current situation, so does the person in his/her pursuit of perfection need, at the beginning of the spiritual journey, a concrete application of principles to his/her situation, particular temperament and disposition.

Spiritual perfection, it is important to remember, takes on many different forms, depending upon the particular circumstances and the variety of conditions that surround each person. Our American culture is surely different from the Spanish culture of the 16th century during the lives of St. Teresa of Avila and St. John of the Cross. St. Thomas More may have been a saint for all seasons but if you were to imitate his style of life and sanctity in our modern setting it would be disastrous for you. You must meet God in your own unique personality and history and avoid any pre-imposed mold of sanctity being put upon you. You need discrimination and discretion for your spiritual growth. Merton put it very well:

> "Many poets are not poets for the same reason that many religious men are not saints: they never succeed in being themselves. They never get around to being the particular poet or the particular monk they are intended to be by God. They never become the man or the artist who is called for by all the circumstances of their individual lives.
>
> They waste their years in vain efforts to be some other poet, some other saint. For many absurd reasons, they are convinced that they are obliged to become somebody else who died two hundred years ago and who lived in circumstances utterly alien to their own.
>
> They wear out their minds and bodies in a hopeless endeavor to have somebody else's experiences or write somebody else's poems or possess somebody else's sanctity."

ADVANTAGES OF SPIRITUAL DIRECTION

Spiritual direction will often prevent us from merely going through the motions of religion.

Many Christians today have almost no idea of God's immense love for them or of the personal nature of that love or of that love's power and ability to bring about a profound fulfillment in their lives. The seeds of spiritual vitality are planted in the heart of every person. But seeds must grow and develop before the harvest can be reaped. Each person needs more than an abstract knowledge of God. He/she needs to know first-hand who God is. Each needs to go through an arduous process of trial and error.

The interior journey is a dangerous one and you ought not to risk traveling it alone. St. Bernard of Clairvaux said that friendship and spiritual direction demand a master other than the disciple for "Who constitutes himself his own master becomes the disciple of a fool." Even if it is a perilous journey you ought not to be frightened. St. Teresa of Avila challenges us:

> "Wouldn't it be nice if while desiring to procure a great treasure I should want to walk without danger along a path where there are so many robbers. For when you are about to gain the treasure—or steal it—since the Lord says that the violent take it away—by a royal road and by a safe road, the road chosen by our King and all His elect and saints, they will tell you that there are so many dangers and so many things to fear. How many more dangers are there for those who think they obtain this good without following a road?"

If spiritual direction only helped you to curb your self-will, it would be invaluable. In fact, your own will often becomes such a burden, such a source of misery and darkness that you will come to have a hunger and thirst for obedience. Merton stresses the need of obedience:

"A spirit that is truly drawn to God in contemplation will soon learn the value of obedience; the hardships and anguish he has to suffer every day from the burden of his own selfishness and clumsiness and incompetence and pride will give him a hunger to be led and advised and directed by somebody else.

His own will becomes the source of so much misery and so much darkness that he does not go to some other man merely to seek light, or wisdom, or counsel; he comes to have a passion for obedience itself and for the renunciation of his will and of his own lights."

But spiritual direction should go far beyond the curbing of self-will. No individual can possibly know himself/herself all alone. Even the best book on discernment is no substitute for the wisdom, prudence and loving care of a good spiritual guide. Such a one will help the directee become his/her best self. Self-deception is easy. The false ego within all of us is busy being biased toward self and prejudiced against others. Self-deception is easy. You are so often fooled since you are so easily ruled by your own defense mechanisms that help you to escape the truth about yourself.

Laziness is magically changed into "an easygoing, not up-tight disposition" while anger and impatience are transformed into "righteous indignation."

SOUL-FRIEND

The title, "spiritual director," seems a bit strange for us moderns. Kenneth Leech in his excellent book, *Soul Friend*, suggests the term, *soul-friend*. The Irish saw it as a necessity to have such a soul-friend.

> "It was seen as necessary for everyone to possess a soul-friend, and the saying, 'Anyone without a soul-friend is a body without a head' (attributed both to Brigit and to Comgall) became an established Celtic proverb ... the soul-friend was essentially a counsellor and guide, and the office was not seen in specifically sacramental terms. Often the soul-friend was a layman or laywoman."

Among the Fathers and Mothers of the eastern deserts the soul-friend, the loving, caring other-self was called a *pneumataphor*, a carrier of the Holy Spirit. The title of *Abbas*, Father, and *Ammas*, Mother, was given to one who shaped the lives of his/her children in the life of the Spirit. Such spiritual "elders" taught by a loving example and not so much from clear and distinct ideas. A saying of the Fathers of the Desert illustrates this:

> "A brother asked Abba Poemen: 'Some brothers live with me. Do you want me to be in charge of them?' The old man said to him: "No, just work first and foremost, and if they want to live like you, they will see to it themselves.' The brother said to him: 'But it is they themselves, Father, who want me to be in charge of them.' The old man said to him: 'No, be their example, not their legislator.''

Such desert elders never conceived their role as spiritual leaders according to the model of a teacher. Basing their role as a spiritual father upon the fatherhood of the Heavenly Father, they experienced something of the self-giving love of the Father within the Trinity toward His Son in His Spirit who bound them together into a oneness of ecstatic love. The close relationship between the leader and the one who is being led was grounded upon the deepest movement of the Spirit, binding the two into a loving relationship that went far beyond any other relationship known in human love, since both persons were striving at every moment to be guided totally by the Spirit. Ideally and actually we should believe from the literature recalling the depth of spiritual progress, that such a school of direction produced two persons who were striving to meet each other at the deepest dimensions of their being, the ground of their being, where God dwells within them.

The saints were such soul-friends to those who came to them to share the workings of the Holy Spirit in both the director and the directee. Such spiritual guides were utterly uncalculating in their self-giving and caring for those whom they sought to help in the spiritual journey. They show us that spiritual direction involves something more than answers to problems, pious clichés and ready-made remedies that were supposed to fit most human beings without consulting the uniqueness of God's working in one's life.

Such a guide accepted a responsibility that could cost heavily since one committed himself/herself to the spiritual growth and the development of a life that fostered eternal, divine life. Each person coming to the soul-friend brought a special personhood and history that the guide had to listen to, that unique working of the Spirit in the disciple. Assurance of prayer and sacrifice on behalf of the directee was a serious undertaking on the part of the director that involved a continued remembrance of the directee before the Lord. Such a loving commitment to the true self of the directee cost the director or soul-friend sacrifice and unselfishness that could only be called a sharing in God's pure love.

Ignace Lepp captures this understanding of "soul-friending:"

> "To meet a master who wishes to become our friend is a great opportunity in life. Thanks to him we shall be able to actualize our principal powers to the maximum. The man who has confidence in himself, far from refusing to be a disciple, freely chooses the master he believes most suited to help him become himself. If there is an art of being a master, there is also an art, scarcely less difficult, of being a disciple. The most effective masters generally began by being excellent disciples. Even Christ began by being baptized, and therefore initiated, by the Precursor."

CHOOSING A SOUL-FRIEND

If you are looking for an individual as your soul-friend, the first quality that you should be looking for is that the director has personally and continually experienced, and is experiencing the dynamics of the spiritual life in order to realize what you are undergoing. Avoid someone who deals in static, pat answers to fit all persons and all situations.

Your director should be a holy, Spirit-filled person who walks in humility and gentleness and is listening with caring love to what the Spirit is doing in your life. He/she is a channel, a mid-wife, bringing you into a new birth in God's Spirit. Such a director lives only to serve and release you into the uniqueness of your true self in God's loving plan.

One should not choose a director by mere natural inclinations but by reason and faith. Besides personal holiness, there should be prudence, experience, learning and a reverence for the mystery of each human being. It is only by faithful attention to God's confident and constant communion with Him, that a soul-friend's guidance will be effective. His loving vision of God, his self-forgetful confidence in God, his desire to give unstintingly for God's purposes, are the source of his energies. He must see to it that he himself is a whole integrated person.

The soul-friend must be daring and decisive but at the same time extremely delicate. He must continually cope with the demands of God and with human weakness. He will need to expend a great deal of time and energy in discerning God's will. In fact, discernment of spirits is right at the heart of soul-friending. The prudent soul-friend will avoid any kind of monopoly or the exploiting of individuals for his own ends. He will never impose his own views and thus diminish the liberty of the human person under the action of the Holy Spirit. Though he must not be crippled by hesitation or undue delay, the prudent soul-friend must be prepared to wait. He must be attuned to God's pace, God's goal, God's manner of moving in the individual's life.

NEED OF EXPERIENCE

It is almost impossible to overestimate the value of experience. Techniques and methods cannot always track down the activity of God in a person. In fact, they may even hinder His action or restrict it if laws of psycho-therapy substitute for the freedom of God's Spirit to move as God wishes to do in the individual directee. There is no substitute for experience. All the masters of the spiritual life have stressed this important quality of a good director. "If a blind man leads another blind man, both fall into the pit." *(Mt 15:14)*.

An inexperienced guide could thwart the spirit's flight or hold it down and even destroy it by imprudent mortifications or an excessive tolerance toward sloth.

Part of his experience should lie in his knowledge, not only of theology and right teaching, but also of the operations of human psychology and the science of the unconscious. St. Teresa of Avila stresses the importance of learning in a good spiritual guide:

"There are opinions going around that learned men if they are not spiritual are no help to people who practice prayer. I have already said that it is necessary to have a spiritual master; but if he is not a learned man, this lack of learning will be a hindrance. It will be a great help to consult with learned men. If they are virtuous even though they may not experience spiritual things, they will benefit me; and God will enable them to explain what they must teach. He will even give them spiritual experience so that they might help us. I do not say this without

101

having experienced it, and it has happened to me with more than two. I say that if a person is going to submit completely to only one master, he would be greatly mistaken if he did not seek one like this . . ."

The soul-friend must regard each individual as sacred and thus stand with reverence before the mystery of each person and the even more fantastic mystery of God in each person. St. John of the Cross is very critical of harsh spiritual guides and compares them to rough blacksmiths who only know how to use the hammer. He reminds them that the real guide of souls is the Holy Spirit.

Since God seldom leads two people by the same route, the soul-friend must be aware of the uniqueness of each person and each path. Untold damage has been done in the past by spiritual directors who have directed with a coldness, a generality that kills any creativity and stifles any originality. The lifeless systems and humorless programs that they have imposed upon the directees under their guidance have robbed these people of the foundation of any greatness or uniqueness. The whole purpose of the soul-friend's instrumentality should be to lead the directee to the degree of holiness where he or she is completely docile to the commands of the ultimate Director, the Holy Spirit.

THE WAY OF LOVE

The art of giving spiritual advice consists for the most part in the ability to establish a rapport between both parties. The relationship between soul-friends is unquestionably a matter of the giving or the withholding of the selves of both. The degree to which both of them are committed to their relationship in the Holy Spirit will determine the success of the whole process. A necessary part of this is an openness of the heart, particularly in time of stress and temptation.

There is only one path that leads into a person's innermost self, effects true healing and gives new creativity unto spiritual life, and that is the way of love. One really knows the other in the only possible way by an experience of union, not by any knowledge that the thoughts can provide. The only real way to full knowledge of another is through loving that other, and this love transcends words or thoughts. No amount of psychological insight can take its place. It can prepare for it, make it possible, even lead to it, but it can never be a substitute for it.

This is like the love of St. Paul when he says that he lives in Christ and that Christ lives in him. Something like this Pauline intimacy with Jesus can be found in the relationships between soul-friends who know and love one another at a very deep level of awareness. Between soul-friends there can develop a union of minds and hearts. This can lead even further to union with Christ Himself. Thus soul-friendship can lead us to Christ-friendship. Soul-friendship with anyone is ultimately Christ-friendship, just as the giving of a cup of water to anyone is like giving a cup of water to Christ. Christ is not divorced from His members. It is not as though one has to jettison all human friendships when a person reaches friendship with Christ.

In your deeper walk with God, it is uplifting

and comforting to travel with "someone along the way." The pilgrimage seems less arduous as you and your soul-friend find your meeting point with Jesus who approaches you and walks with you. What wonderment and joy to discover the Triune God more intimately and more fully when as His two disciples you go forth together to seek Him. Just as the two disciples on the road to Emmaus felt their hearts burning inside of them as Jesus explained the Scriptures to them, so too do you meet Him more intimately as you pray and share with each other. You are guided, inspired and led by the risen Lord to turn around and set your heart and mind on your final destination, the Heavenly Jerusalem, where you will see Him face to face.

"The throne of God and of the Lamb shall be there, and his servants shall serve him faithfully. They shall see him face to face, and bear his name on their foreheads. The night shall be no more. They will need no light from lamps or the sun, for the Lord God shall give them light, and they shall reign forever," *(Rev. 22:3-5)*.

8

Prayer is a Loving Presence

God so loved this world that He gave us His only begotten Son so that we would believe in Him and experience His closeness and oneness with us, in order that we might not "perish" but have everlasting life *(Jn 3:16)*.

This is the incredibly good news that God is a God "toward us" and for us. If God is love by His nature *(1 JN 4:8)*, then He activates that love by wishing to share His very being with us intimately as an abiding presence.

> If anyone loves me he will keep my word,
> and my Father will love him,
> and we shall come to him
> and make our home with him   *(Jn 14:23)*.

BEING A PRESENT TO OTHERS

It is quite natural that you think of giving presents to your loved ones and friends. What is a present except your desire to extend yourself through the symbol of the gift into the *being* of the other? You are saying in the gift given: "I want to be a *presence* of self-giving to you. Accept me, please, as a part of your life, your well-being, your happiness."

God says that to us in the feast of Christmas, the Incarnation. He now, as a trinitarian family, can be forever "God among us"—Emmanuel, through Jesus Christ. God has pitched His tent among us *(Jn 1:14)* and now in Jesus Christ will forever be a living and infinitely loving presence to us.

The mystery of being a *presence* to another admits of many levels of self-giving to the other. You have surely experienced many times the movement from absence toward presence as you met a stranger on a plane, train or wherever providence brought you, into the possibility of a further growth into your own human *being*, and allowed a stranger to discover in your openness a bit more of his or her *being*. So often on your journey through life you find yourself next to people whom you have never met before. They sit close to you. But they are "objects" next to you, "over there," until one smiles, says a kind word of interest to the other. The mystery of presence begins when one becomes "present" in his/her words and gestures that communicate the mysterious message that says: "I do not know you. We are closed to each other. But I would like to be open for you. Let's be mutually available to each other."

Such a mystery of presence cannot be forced nor can it be understood and willed for any pragmatic motive. Just as we could not force God to give us His Son, Jesus Christ, so we cannot force any human person to gift us with his/her love. This gift of presence admits of various levels of becoming present to the other as two people move away from the controlled object-object relationship into the movement of one toward the other as toward a possible other-self. *Availability* is the act by which you incline yourself freely to be a presence to another.

Being a presence toward another admits of great intensity, depending on how unselfishly you wish to give yourself in loving service to the other in both affective and effective love. Passing acquaintances usually do not develop into deep presences. For the development of deep presence between two persons, time and intimate sharing are necessary. Deep love presence is rooted in a desire to live for the other's complete good and happiness. You would do anything to bring to actuality the complete fulfillment of the other.

AN I-THOU MUTUALITY

Such a love presence takes place secondly in a *mutuality*, in an *I-Thou* relationship as two interchange the gift of each other. Such a presence is intensified as you do not selfishly look for anything in return; yet there is a mutual gifting which becomes all the stronger when you forget about the returned gift and concentrate only on the gift of yourself.

REALIZING THE EXCHANGE

Thirdly, presence demands an actualization of the exchange. Presence that is not experienced as self-gifting in a coming together will become an absence if never renewed in self-giving. There is always a need for communion or sharing the oneness in spirit. Here presence increases as you

empty all, both the good and even the weaknesses, in trusting, self-gifting revelation of
yourself in the most intimate, deepest levels of
sharing your total "person" with another.

GOD'S PRESENCE TO US

We have been discussing in various ways that
God is love by His nature and that, therefore, He
is also "presence" as self-giving by His very
nature. But in what way can you and I experience
God's presence to us? How can you live to make
God happy? How can God who is so completely
perfect and immutable receive anything from you
that would add anything to His personhood? Does
God really wish to share His being with you to the
degree of "communion," where you truly can
become one with Him?

God's Word became flesh and dwelt among us
in the person of Jesus Christ to invite you to
receive the gift of God's very being in the most intimate friendship. God establishes in Jesus Christ
through His death and resurrection the New
Covenant whereby God pledges Himself not only to share with you His gifts for your happiness,
but to commit Himself in the gift of Himself to
you for your total happiness. " . . . but he (God)
does it all for your own good, so that you may
share his own holiness" (Heb. 12:10).

God pours into your heart His love through the
Spirit whom He gives you (Rm. 5:5) and who
dwells within you (Rm. 8:9) in order that in His
Spirit you might know that you are truly a child
of God (1 Jn 3:1), made an heir with Christ of
Heaven forever (Rm. 8:17). Jesus is the way, the
truth and the life who leads you into the most in-

timate presence of the Trinity who wishes effectively to come and abide within you, Father, Son and Spirit (Jn. 14:23).

God wishes to give you His presence of availability for your complete happiness in your awareness of your eternal sonship and daughtership within His family, so that you too can live unto God's happiness, glory and praise. You praise God most when you live consciously in Christ in order that with His mind you may glorify the Father in His Spirit of love.

A MUTUAL SHARING

You too can share yourself with God when at every moment you seek with Jesus to do God's holy will. This was Jesus' mutual self-gift back to the Father from whom he received the gift of the Father. You can also enter into a mutual sharing with God. God lives within you and raises you up by His free gift of Himself in His uncreated energies of love (grace), divinizing you into participators in His very own nature (2 P 1:4). By God's gratuitous self-gift you are made worthy to receive His fullness of presence, His availability toward you for your complete happiness. " . . . because my aim is to do not my own will, but the will of him who sent me" (Jn. 5:30).

Desire to share yourself with God who shares Himself, Father, Son and Holy Spirit, so perfectly and completely, he prompts you to seek at all times to live in greater awareness of your communication with God as He gives you His Word. How you ought to burn with desire never to lose this consciousness of being one with God, communing at each moment in the events of your life

109

with God as your Ultimate Source and End of your very being! You wish to live in love more consciously as you are aware of your oneness in God's communicating love. You are ready to put to death everything that impedes the new life lived in communion with the Trinity. "Every thought is our prisoner, captured to be brought into obedience to Christ. Once you have given your complete obedience, we are prepared to punish any disobedience" *(2 Co 10:5)*.

LIVE AS YOU PRAY

There is a basic law of growth in prayer that applies also to your level of growth in your development as mature human persons. Look at a small child praying and you will know where that child is in the long journey toward full personhood. The child is present to God only when it feels a need. God is fashioned out of basic needs on the part of the child. God is the great Santa Claus. God is infinitely present in self-giving love to the child, but is perceived in the child's prayer only as a presence of a Giver.

As you personally develop through adolescence into early adulthood in experiencing yourself more and more in availability, mutuality and in the actualization of your self-giving to others in your human relationships, so you can open up to God and be present to Him in greater availability, mutuality and actual true exchange of yourself with His being.

So you see—as you live, so you pray. And as you pray, so you live. But now can we not say: as you are present to loved ones in an intimate presence of an *I-Thou* in genuine self-giving love, so you become present to God in the same way? God's love as presence is being actuated or incarnated when you love another human being. Is this not the meaning of the two key texts in the first epistle of John?

No one has ever seen God;
but as long as we love one another
God will live in us
and his love will be complete in us   *(1 Jn 4:12)*

God is love
and anyone who lives in love lives in God,
and God lives in him   *(1 Jn. 4:16)*.

LIVING IN LOVE

The presence of God within you becomes a swelling ocean wave that seeks to burst through the space of your heart to flow out and inundate the entire world before you with God's love. You whisper the name and presence of Father, Son and Holy Spirit over your world. What was hidden now becomes revealed, what was absent now through your cooperation becomes present.

The presence of God experienced as intimate love within you becomes a presence of God as transforming love around you. You are called to intimacy by living in the indwelling presence of God. But such intimacy finds its fullness in the *birthing* of God's loving presence in others whom you are sent to serve with love.

Intimate love begets other intimate loves. A loving community gives birth to new loving communities. And you find your happiness and fulfillment, as God does, in becoming progressively more open and available to beget others into their unique happiness as they discover their *I-ness* in the *Thou* of your gift of self.

RELEASING GOD'S PRESENCE IN THE WORLD

You have moved from being closed to being open to God and you become intensely aware of God communing with you at all times with His infinite love within you. You wish at all times to pray as you seek in all things to love with your whole heart and with all your strength *(Dt 6:6)*. You are also driven outward toward the world in which you live. You wish to share your new-founded *being*, discovered in God's great love for you. It is always a movement, therefore, outward toward those human beings around you. You go to become God's presence of love toward all whom you are privileged to meet, and you become available to them to call them into their being through the mystery of your unique presence.

God's presence is infinite; His love is total and complete. Yet the experience of God's presence is quite dependent on you and me to release His love in the context of our human situation. God calls others into being by His love in us, shown in genuine, loving presence to those others. I witnessed this call into presence the other day—a call that is always a *becoming*, an unending series of being birthed into new being. After con-celebrating a beautiful *Liturgy*, I observed one of the concelebrating priests turn to one of the little acolytes to ask his name. "John, it was a real privilege to be on the altar today with you," the priest told the boy with great sincerity. It was a genuine openness to the *I* in that young boy. The priest was God's presence to him in that moment as the boy understood that he was important in the eyes of that priest. That boy could better understand now that he was also beautiful in the eyes of God Himself.

TENSIONED LIVING

Yet why are you and I not capable of being God's presence to others at all times? Why are we not more present to God throughout the day? One difficulty lies in the tension between the inner, living experience of the indwelling Trinity and the outward giving of that love and new life to others. It is a tension between the eternal *now* experienced in those moments of aloneness with the *Alone* and this present temporal *now* that is so full of the absence of love and openness in self-giving to others. There is a tension and brokenness that more easily separates contemplation from daily living than unites them into the same presence of love for God and neighbor.

Another reason is that we Western Christians tend to separate spirit and matter, God and His material creation. Distinction should not be the same as separation. For those who have the eyes to see, God is everywhere present, inserted into His material creation and working to bring it into its fulfillment unto His glory and the sharing of His own life and happiness with His human creatures. The divine presence through the physical, created world assails us, penetrates and moulds us. God shouts out from inside of each material moment in space and time that He is here present and this place is holy by His presence as an activating, loving energy. God is revealing Himself everywhere, through our groping efforts, as a universal milieu, an environment, the air that we breathe. All beings have full reality and are holy in proportion as they converge upon this Ultimate Point. God is the source of all perfections and the goal toward which created beings are moving in an *elan vital* to their completion.

This vision of worshipful communion between you and your Divine Creator, whereby you can lose yourself in God as in an "Other," is grounded in the Word Incarnate, Jesus Christ. In Him, as St. Paul teaches with such insistence, all things are reunited and are consummated. By the resurrectional presence of Christ who fills all things the whole of creation has a meaningful consistency.

VIRGIN AND MOTHER OF GOD

That is why the archetype of the Church and of us Christians from earliest centuries has always been Mary, virgin and mother of God. It is not enough to realize in prayer throughout the day and night that you have been chosen by God's predilection to be His spouse, a pure and empty virgin with no power but the power of awe-ful expectancy to receive the triune God's gift of indwelling, intimate love. You are called to be mother to the life and presence of God in the world around you.

9

Surrender in the Now Moment

We have hopefully followed Yahweh's injunction: "Be still and know I am your God" *(Ps 46:10)*. Stilling the noises within our hearts that cry out from the depths of our false ego, we have honestly been waiting attentively to hear God speak His healing Word.

Yet healing comes not only through God's Word found in Scripture. The Word of God is a two-edged sword that cleaves the soul, our human way of thinking, from the Spirit, the way God thinks *(Heb 4:12)*. That Word, Jesus Christ, is operating with His Spirit of love at every moment in the context of our human situation. What has been revealed in Scripture is meant to be experienced in our daily lives.

But concretely your daily life unfolds only moment by moment. And the only moment you have as God's gifted time and place to meet Him and surrender to His loving activity is this *now* moment. You are meant to know the importance of your human situation, made up of so many pleasant and unpleasant moments, of so much darkness and light, of so many fears and also of loves.

We become contemplatives in a process of continued growth by "seeing" God unveiling His loving self-giving to us in this *now* moment and then in the same moment joyfully saying *yes* in returned self-surrender. May you and I learn the importance of embracing fully the richness of the present *now* moment and in that "place" that is holy because God is present as giving love, learn to give ourselves completely back to Him in loving adoration and service to others.

The best word to describe true Christian contemplation is the word "surrender." Contemplation is a continued process of experiencing God's infinite surrendering love to you and your return by the surrender of your entire being to God in love. But where are you to discover God in His continued act of surrendering love to you except in the context of your daily life, in this present *now* moment? What moment will be the most apt and acceptable time in which you can surrender yourself in returned love, other than the present moment *now*?

God's love for you is constant, infinite and unchanging. His uncreated energies enfold you with a sameness that is eternal. God speaks to you from His everlasting, immutable, faithful *now* momentless moment that embraces all moments of our earthly time. "I have loved you with an everlasting love, so I am constant in my affection for you" *(Jr 31:3)*. The Heavenly Father truly loves you, Jesus said *(Jn 16:27)*.

That love unfolds and meets you in the *now* situation in which you find yourself, an uncreated love that never changes; that bursts out always in new and surprising ways as God, Trinity, enters into your daily needs and counts all the hairs of your head *(Lk 12:7)* and meets all of your needs when you ask for them with the mind of Christ *(Jn 14:13; Jn 15:7)*.

From our point of view the inbreaking of God's loving providence yesterday and last year and years earlier is different in its manifestations. The past, as fast-moving water in a mountain stream, is precisely past from this present moment. It has passed you by and enriched you if you surrendered in that moment that once was the *now* encounter point of your contemplating God in His unfolding love. The future moments are hiding behind the clouds of the not-yet and the possible. Perhaps only one future moment of yesterday will be the moment of this *now* or this moment may be a surprise unplanned or unexpected by you as you gazed into the future.

THE REAL MOMENT IS *NOW*

Blaise Pascal in a well-known text comments on how we live under fear of the past or the future and thus lose the only contact we have with reality:

"We never hold ourselves to the present time. We anticipate the future as coming too slowly in order to hasten its advent. Or we recall the past in order to stop its passage too rapidly. Too imprudently we err in times which are not ours and we do not think

117

of what only is in our power, what truly does belong to us.

So in vain do we hanker for those things which are no more and thus we let fly away, without batting an eyelash, the only thing that exists. This is the present which ordinarily wounds us. We hide it from view because it afflicts us. And if it is pleasing to us, we regret seeing it pass."

True contemplation is God's gift given to you in the Spirit's infused gifts of faith, hope and love that allow you to enter into the richness of each moment to adore, love and surrender to God, Father, Son and Holy Spirit. A contemplative is a gifted human being, a "seer" capable of seeing into God's real world.

With such a gift you can see God in Holy Scripture, in the history of salvation and see the same God operating in your present human situation. You see the love of God incarnated in Jesus Christ who now is gloriously risen and inserted by His living presence into every atom of the material world that surrounds you at every moment. You see this Jesus of Nazareth still multiplying the loaves, the Bread of Life, and giving Himself as food and drink in the Eucharist. You see Him within the Church, the people of God bound by the Holy Spirit's love in a community of service to extend Jesus Christ as the Light of the world. You see Him also in the teaching authority within the Church.

You learn daily to see Him in each person whom you meet, in each human activity and event of each day. Jesus Christ is shining diaphanously throughout the whole world for those who have the contemplative eyes of faith, hope and love to see Him, as Teilhard de Chardin in his *Divine Milieu* writes. You shout out your exciting discoveries of Jesus becoming incarnated again and again in the world around you as Mary and the shepherds of Bethlehem did. You share your gift of contemplative faith by instructing others as to how to have their spiritual eyes opened to see God as you are beginning to do.

THE EVENT

In such a Christian vision process you find God working in all things by His grace, His uncreated energies, touching you and drawing you always into a more intimate union with Himself. It is a contemplative vision that takes you from darkness and places you fully in the light of God's loving presence as the Ground not only of your very being but of that of all creatures. It is a true "unconcealment," an uncovering of what is always there; but through lack of faith we are kept from fully communicating with the ever-present and ever-loving God. He is totally present to and perfectly loving us. Are we present in each event and at each moment to God?

Faith, the work of the energizing Holy Spirit, removes before our eyes, like scales that fall away, the false masks from others and from ourselves. In a gentle security of knowing you are loved by the all-perfect God, you can let go of your need to interpret events or happenings according to darkened ideas that you may have been entertaining, especially from out of your false *ego*. You and I, because we do not have faith strong enough to convince us of God's love for us unto death in His Son Jesus, fashion opinions of ourselves and the world around us that are simply lies and do not present the "really real" as God sees it.

The event is, therefore, whatever is happening to you. The word is derived from the Latin word, *evenire*, to come out of. It dynamically presents you with a given moment out of which something is coming, being brought to birth. By faith you can say that God is coming out of this or that moment as your loving God. What is happening in this *now* moment is that God is calling you to find Him in this happening moment. It is not as if God has been sleeping and He now wakes up and "comes out" of the event as a butterfly emerges from the darkness of the cocoon. God has been there all the time, loving and giving Himself in the moments that preceded and prepared this moment. It is you and I who have to come out of our sleep and wake up to the reality of God's loving presence in each moment and in each event of our human situation.

We have been unaware of the richness of God's love in those preceding moments, going all the way back to our birth. Now faith stirs us to awaken to God's inner presence inside the materiality of this moment. From your side, you go *into* the event, you discover by a finding inside the event what was already there. As God comes out of *(evenire)*, you go into *(invenire)*, and there in the given moment the loving union of two wills becoming one that we can call contemplation takes place.

In each event of each moment God is calling

you into reality out of your shadowy existence. Your greatest work in life is the asceticism of listening to God's call with utter openness and sincerity. It is a receptive readiness to swing freely wherever God leads. "Speak, Lord, thy servant hears" *(1 S 3:10)*. Your most difficult ascetical struggle comes in what the Fathers of the Desert call *nepsis*, the constant, interior vigilance you are to exercise over every thought, feeling, imagination *(2 Co 10:5)* that could possibly throw you out of the faith dimension of being in Christ, back into the darkness of insecurity and fear of your false ego.

In each event you discover by a new, positive awareness that you really are a child of God *(1 Jn 3:1)*. You learn in the event to let go of negativity and you find the godly and the truthful in each moment. You learn to yield gently to God's loving presence in yourself so that you think and act as whole and healed, for that is what God sees you to be already in His love for you. Aggressiveness against others disappears as you gently let the presence of God come forth. With Mary you utter at each moment: "I am the handmaid of the Lord. Let what you have said be done to me" *(Lk 1:38)*. God in you meets the God in others and you discover the freeing joy that the Spirit has made you and them one in Christ.

THE PRESENT MOMENT

You cannot become who you are already in God's love except in the present moment that God is handing to you, as the sacred "place" to take off your shoes of security and fall down and worship

Him before the burning bush. "Take off your shoes, for the place on which you stand is holy ground" *(Ex 3:5)*. For you as a faith-full Christian seeking the face of God in each event, it is this present moment in which you find a new incarnation of God's self-giving love to you. Or perhaps it would be more true to say that God is again taking on "flesh", breaking into your world to pitch His tent with you, to bring His *Shekinah* or infinite glory into your darkened world. Or simply you could say that Jesus is being "unconcealed for you," for, since His first incarnation, death and resurrection, He has never really left you.

In this present moment God and you meet in the Incarnate Word, Jesus Christ, as Teilhard de Chardin writes "by the game of the resurrection." Jesus Christ is caught forever by a new presence inside matter. He touches it and reconciles it back to the Father through you and me finding in this present moment what the Father has eternally seen in His loving Word. The historical time of this *now* moment (in Greek, the *chronos*) is carried over by the eternal *now* of God's healing (salvific time, the *kairos*). God's grace in His uncreated energies of love touches your free will and the Body-Being of His only begotten Son, Jesus Christ, is extended again into space and time.

THE SACRAMENT OF THE PRESENT MOMENT

If God is "inside" the stuff of each moment, He must be effecting what these signs are symbols of—His great self-giving love toward us. J.P. de Caussade, in his classical work *Abandonment to*

Divine Providence, gives us the very suggestive phrase: "the sacrament of the present moment." Sacraments are visible signs made up of material things and gestures along with words that lead Christians, not only into what the signs signify, but also into an effective encounter with Jesus Christ who brings about by His Holy Spirit what the signs signify.

Through your faith that God is creatively present in each moment, you can, therefore, believe that He is in an analogous way effecting a sacramental self-giving to the Christian, thus bringing you into a greater union with Himself. In the sacrament of the Holy Eucharist the priest breathes over bread and wine the words: "This is My Body . . . This is My Blood." Through the calling down of the Holy Spirit, the faithful enter into an "unconcealment" to find that these gifts are no longer mere bread and wine; a transfiguration has taken place. This is now the Body and Blood of Jesus Christ.

Also in the context of your Christian life the Holy Spirit gives you faith to see the Body of Christ in an analogous way being formed, or better, being revealed in the event of each moment. You can thus reverence and adore His sacred presence wherever you find yourself. As you surrender to His loving activity, God's Spirit reveals to you what Jesus has effected in the primal eucharistic gift of Himself to you on the cross. In faith, hope and love with which you encounter God in each moment, you can joyfully relinquish control over your life, plans, desires for this moment. In total abandonment, you yield to God's dynamic, loving activity in this *now* event.

A LIVING, ACTIVE FAITH

It is not enough to open yourself to God's gift to you in the present moment. Contemplation is more than merely "seeing" God and worshipping Him. By faith you "see" God, get in touch with His loving activities and then work with Him in loving service to effect a transformation into something even better. Faith illumines you in a freeing way to see God inside of the moment. But there is a freeing by faith also from yourself and the limitations that you and I so readily place upon ourselves and others. The negativity that believes you and others can do only so much is transcended by faith so that you can truly shout out to yourself and to the whole world: "I can do all things in Him who strengthens me."

Faith does not lead you into presumption but into a true assessment of each situation and what you can do with God's help to change matters according to God's will. True gentleness and meekness are rooted in humility, in seeing reality through faith according to God's eyes. You can turn the other cheek to your enemies but God would want you also to work diligently at the same time to transform them by your love and prayerful intercession into your brothers and sisters. Faith works along with God's gift of human intelligence, but it allows you to see farther into the tunnel when your own human knowledge runs out of light.

Faith to believe in God's infinite love is rooted in the Word of God. You learn through the illumination of the Holy Spirit to have an uncompromising openness to God's call in the history of salvation. It is through openness to Holy Scripture that we are able to enter into a faith act that convinces us that Jesus Christ is still speaking to us. Our faith in the Good News and His healing power breaking in upon us through the event of the present moment comes from a prayerful knowledge of Scripture.

CONTEMPLATION IS PRAYING ALWAYS

Ultimately abandoning yourself to God in the event of each moment brings you into a state of infused prayer that allows you to "pray incessantly," as St. Paul says *(1 Th 5:18)*. You live in a constant remembrance of God in His loving self-giving to you in each moment. Because the Holy Spirit is pouring into your heart deeper faith, hope and love, you can thank God for all things because you will be able to see His loving presence and active goodness in each creature that comes into your life. Thanking Him for all things at all times, you will be always united in prayerful adoration and praise. "Praise Yahweh, my soul! I mean to praise Yahweh all my life, I mean to sing to my God as long as I live" *(Ps 146: 1-2)*. You believe that God is "righteous in all that he does. Yahweh acts only out of love" *(Ps 145:17)*.

The sign of a constant praying attitude in each event is the lack of excessive worries and the presence of a rejoicing heart. "I want you to be happy, always happy in the Lord; I repeat, what I want is your happiness. Let your tolerance be evident to everyone: the Lord is near. There is no need to worry . . . " *(Ph 4:4-5)*. Not only will you find God in each moment, but you will in each

125

moment respond to His loving presence. The Eucharist is God's gift of Himself totally to you in His Son Jesus through His Spirit. In your daily life, each moment is the "place" where you return your eucharistic gift of yourself to God. This place, this *now* event, is holy, for God's holy presence as love to you is unveiled there. It is holy because you respond by the power of the Holy Spirit to become God's holy child.

Trust in Yahweh and do what is good;
make your home in the land and live in peace;
make Yahweh your only joy
and he will give you what your heart desires.
Commit your fate to Yahweh,
trust in him and he will act   *(Ps 37:3-5)*.

10

Contemplation as a Stretching Out Toward God

Life is a journey and we are constantly taking to the road again! A tune comes to our lips. There is a spring to our walk as we set our eyes on the goal again. It is great to be alive! And part of that *joie de vivre* is to stretch out with open arms to embrace life and more abundance of that life. That is why Jesus came among us and why He pours out His Spirit upon us that we might have His life and have it more abundantly *(Jn 10:10)*.

We know from our daily experiences shared with our loved ones that love begets love, desire for greater love begets greater desire. Simply put, the more we hunger for God, the more we hunger for God! Blaise Pascal once wrote that all we can really give God is *desire*. Let us desire with desire to journey more deeply into our hearts and there surrender more completely to God's Word, Jesus Christ, dwelling within us with His Father in their mutual Spirit of love. Let us stretch out toward God in greater consciousness of loving union. Stretching is the sign of a pilgrim in the desert moving with joyful haste to go to Mount Zion, to meet his God in the Temple of the Heavenly Jerusalem. It is also a realistic acceptance of who we are in our historical situation and to stretch in and through those very circumstances to find God in the next step ahead.

In our modern world you and I are experiencing constantly the cry from within ourselves to discover ourselves more and more as unique persons, capable of loving others more intimately and being loved more personally by them. There is now a great need in our de-humanizing society for an "I-Thou," a person-to-person confrontation and mutual sharing within our families, among friends and above all in our prayerful relations with God.

We have engaged in past time in a great deal of repetitious, formal prayer, especially in our liturgical and communal prayers. But today the person is important. You feel that you must be free, free to say your "yes" to God and really mean it. You see that there can be no separation between your prayer-life and your life on the horizontal level of relating to those around you. And so you in your prayer-life feel the need to get down deeper into your intimate self, into that which the Eastern Christian writers as well as those who wrote Scripture call the "heart". This refers as a symbol to that complexity which is not merely your physical heart but is the totality of your being. Standing before God who is the ground of your being, you look up into His face and say, "Yes! I surrender!" This is the type of total prayer that we are searching for today.

The following familiar example is used to illustrate how we live on different levels of our being: A lake admits of different levels. There is the surface, the rock formation of the lake, the flora, the mud; all are parts of the lake, but these are not quite that which gives to the lake its "lake-ness." That spring bubbling new life into the lake is the source of the lake's being.

In you and me there are the various levels of the senses, emotions, affections, whose reactions often have been predetermined through heredity, education and social conditioning. All are parts of you, the existential you that makes you to be you. But still, somehow or other, it is not the real you. You can go down deeper and deeper into the pit of your being until you hit the "bottom." Here you are most free, away from the pre-determinations of the senses and the emotions, of your past hurting and painful memories, free to truly confront God and say "yes" to Him with your very being and not merely with some part of your sense life, not with simple words alone or pious sentiments flowing out of your emotional life.

Even though the "cave" within you be in utter dryness and darkness, yet you call up the whole of your being to respond to God, not once in prayer, but as a continuous state of being. You maintain a constant attitude, a burning desire within your "heart", your consciousness infused by the Spirit's faith, hope and love, to stretch out in the totality of your being in self-surrendering love to God. When such a stretching toward God becomes habitual and penetrates every thought, word and deed, you could be called a "contemplative." Prayer is then not so much a thing you do or words you say. God does not need such things from you. He wishes the gift of yourself so that in your surrender of yourself to Him you can find complete happiness as you live in love of God and neighbor. This is a state of being in communication and communion with God as the ultimate ground of your total being.

I have earlier described contemplation as basically a look turned toward God in faith, hope and love. It is you standing, as it were, outside of the habitual idea that you have both of yourself and of God. It is getting down below that false ego and reaching into your deepest source where you stand naked before God, consciously turning toward Him as your Source, your Origin in loving surrender.

This looking upon God is, therefore, the essential act of contemplation. It does not consist in having beautiful thoughts, nor in having any emotions, sentiments or piety. It consists fundamentally in standing before God, not with one faculty perceiving some facet of God but with your total being absorbed into the total being of God. It is heart speaking to heart. It is the return of your whole being back to God as a gift that expresses the attitude which we could call worship-prayer, the ultimate point of true love which is called contemplation.

A DIALOGUE IN BEING

True contemplation cannot be found solely in the "give me, give me, Lord," of petition, nor even in thanksgiving nor even in expiation or sorrow. But it must ultimately overwhelm you in your praise, because you understand from an experience infused into you by the Spirit of God what it means to be a created gift out of God's personalized love. You begin humbly to understand through faith, hope and love what it means to belong to God. Jesus put it succinctly: "The Father truly loves you" *(Jn 16:27)*.

God is more intimate to you than you are to yourself, as St. Augustine wrote in the 4th century. The Trinity of Divine Persons, Father, Son and Spirit, live within you and are loving you infinitely at every moment. Nothing can ever separate you from the infinite love of God. This experience can come only in contemplation and you cannot reach this by your own natural powers alone. Only God can reveal Himself to you in a free offering just as only you can surrender yourself freely in love to your best friend.

Thus contemplation is in the form of a dialogue, but one on the level of being. It is not just a banal conversation. You can spend long hours talking to God. You say this; then it's God's turn to say His part. His part can all too often be what you want God to say. Such a conversation is stacked in your favor, usually toward your "carnal mind," as St. Paul describes a person not consciously surrendered to the moving presence of the Holy Spirit in prayer *(Rm 8:26-27)*. You can spend years in this sort of prayer and it does not perceptibly change your personality.

Does your prayer give you an immersion, an assimilation into God in which you truly understand that you live, no longer you yourself, but God lives in you? *(Ga 2:20)*. This immersion in God can come only from contemplation, the gift of the Spirit, not from a banal conversation directed by the world's greatest movie director, one's own false ego!

Thus your dialogue with God in prayer must participate in some type of intimate, real relationship that touches the core of your being, not just your intellect, not just emotions or good sentiments, as would a prayer that might be empty of involvement of being. Contemplation involves your whole being and changes your life in your depths, bringing about a continuous stretching out in a process of growth in surrendering yourself completely to God's direction.

True contemplation is pushing yourself under the movement of God's Spirit toward God as the totally Other and yet as the indwelling Ground of your entire being. In such a state of being, you grow and yet such a growth admits of an infinity of growth. "Eye has not seen, nor ear heard . . . nor has it entered into the mind of man to conceive what God has prepared for those who love Him . . . " *(1 Co 2:9)*. You are what you truly are before God through a gift from God, but it is a gift that is an ongoing process that calls for your constant desire to grow and receive more of God within your consciousness.

Every time you breathe, God is giving forth His Word in you. And so you want to return this gift by that complete openness to God that looks into His face and says: "Yes, I am at Your service. Be it done to me according to Your Word." Love must be proved by deeds and the deed is precisely this attitude of complete service toward God who first has loved you and whose Spirit drives you out in loving service to your neighbor.

THE JOURNEY OF CONTEMPLATION

If you wish then to start out in search of God on the long, curving road of contemplation, you may feel that you are throwing yourself into the pursuit of the unknowable; that you have only in your favor your great desire to pursue God up the mountain as Moses climbed up Mount Sinai to encounter God in the dark cloud of unknowing. Even this desire has been given you by the Holy Spirit who comes to your weakness when you do not know how to pray as you ought *(Rm 8: 26:27)*. But God hides this fact from you. You think at least you can give Him this desire, you can stretch out in hunger and thirst to possess God, but even this has come from God.

The important thing now as you begin your journey is to desire to listen to God. You want to know Him deeply as person, not as a concept. You wish to destroy the idol you have been creating and call your God. You want to meet the living God of Abraham, Isaac and Jacob. But He can only be met in the desert of your own being, in the depths where you encounter God in your dread of loss. So few of us have the courage to discipline ourselves, to cut ourselves off from all the attachments that build up our self-centeredness, to go out into the desert and be at the mercy of God.

Using the beautiful description of St. Gregory of Nyssa of the 4th century in his classic on Christian mysticism, *Life of Moses*, you set off on this search for God and begin ascending the great mountain. You prepare your bags, you saddle up the donkey and set off on the road. You set off at daybreak and it is a great departure. You are saying goodby. To whom? To what? In a way, to everything and yet, in a way, to nothing. To everything, because you must be a pilgrim stripped of all things and you must let God, the Ground of your being, expose Himself to you as He wishes.

And yet you are not cutting yourself off from anything, because on that donkey you are putting your past history, your intelligence, your imagination, all your weaknesses along with your strengths. You are not throwing off the person that you existentially are for some ideal that you would like to be, for some rarified angel. God is going to meet you in the desert of your existential history with all its brokenness. And so you take along with you on this road of contemplation all that you are.

MOVEMENT FROM DARKNESS TO LIGHT

All Christian mystics, beginning with the Father of Christian mysticism, St. Gregory of Nyssa, describe to us how the movement toward enlightenment begins in the darkness of our brokenness and sin. The pilgrim, like Moses as he began his ascent of Mount Sinai, begins in the darkness of sin. You see a ray of the light of God which beckons you to leave the foothills and start climbing upward. The higher stages are degrees of your entrance into another darkness, that of God's incomprehensibility.

St. Gregory in his *Commentary on the Song of Songs* well describes this higher form of darkness:

" . . . our initial withdrawal from wrong and erroneous ideas of God is a transition from darkness to light. Next comes a closer awareness of hidden things, and by this the soul is guided through sense phenomena to the world of the invisible. And this awareness is a kind of cloud, which overshadows all appearances, and slowly guides and accustoms the soul to look towards what is hidden. Next the soul makes progress through all these stages and goes on higher, and as she leaves behind all that human nature can attain, she enters within the secret chamber of the divine knowledge, and here she is cut off on all sides by the divine darkness. Now she leaves outside all that can be grasped by sense or by reason, and the only thing left for her contemplation is the invisible and the incomprehensible."

You experience in contemplation a triple movement that has a spiral effect which moves you from lower to higher levels of experience of God. This is a cyclical movement from darkness to light to shadow and back again to darkness, to begin again; but now in a higher consciousness and greater oneness with God.

EPECTASIS—A STRETCHING FORTH

I shall always be grateful to the insight that Origen and St. Gregory of Nyssa, his disciple, gave me which I would like to share with you in this teaching on contemplation as a process of stretching more and more toward God. Their key insight is that the love of God in us is a force expanding our being and making us infinitely capable of possessing God in an unending process of greater growth. St. Gregory describes true perfection as "never to stop growing towards what is better and never to place any limit on perfection."

I am so relieved that heaven won't be an old-folks' home! There are no old people in Heaven, but only persons always becoming younger and younger as they stretch out in loving service to become the whole universe as they discover in contemplation God at the heart of all His creation, especially in the imageness of Himself that He has placed within the heart of all human persons.

Grace, or the life of God within you, both in this life and in the life to come, presupposes growth in accepting a loving relationship with God and implies the necessity of constantly moving toward God. St. Gregory writes: "Seeing that it is of the nature of Goodness to attract those who raise their eyes towards it, the soul keeps rising ever higher and higher."

St. Gregory gives us two reasons, always viable for all human beings for all time, why our progress toward God can never come to an end. The first reason is that Beauty, God Himself, is infinite. The second reason is that the Beautiful is of such a nature that the desire for it can never be fully satisfied. He writes: "The soul that looks up towards God and conceives that good desire for His eternal beauty, constantly experiences an ever new yearning for that which lies ahead and her desire is never given its full satisfaction."

God has implanted within you the seed according to His own image and likeness to be developed until—but then, it will never reach an *until*, according to St. Gregory. When can you love God enough, the Supreme Beauty? Can you ever experience enough of love when that love is God Himself? This stretching out to possess ever more the Unpossessable God is not a sadness or a frustration but it fills you with joy and youthfulness. Contemplation is ever more the deepening of your consciousness and experience "that the true satisfaction of your desire consists in constantly going on with your quest and never ceasing in your ascent to God, seeing that every fulfillment of your desire continually generates a further desire for the Transcendent."

St. Gregory takes the Greek word, *epectasis* from St. Paul to describe the Christian's constant state of stretching always more and more toward God.

I can assure you, my brothers, I am far from thinking that I have already won. All I can say is that I forget the past and I strain ahead for what is still to come; I am racing for the finish, for the prize to which God calls us upwards to receive in Christ Jesus *(Ph. 3:13)*.

God as Love is limitless. Our desire to possess also should be limitless. This is the work of the Holy Spirit. St. Gregory puts it succinctly: ". . . for it may be that human perfection consists precisely in this constant growth in the good." Such a stretching forth to higher perfection, greater assimilation into the Absolute, is a motion toward greater being and yet is also a state of stability, of entering into the seventh day of God's rest. Motion for St. Gregory and for the true contemplative means more than moving from one stage to another of perfection. The very transcendence of God is the reason that perfection itself is constant motion. God is eternally at rest; yet He exists always in an outgoing motion of love to share Himself with the other.

Thus as God purifies you of all taint of self-absorption, He draws you continually to "keep rising ever higher and higher, stretching with its desire for heavenly things to those that are before *(Ph 3:13)*, as the Apostle Paul tells us, and thus it will always continue to soar ever higher . . . And thus the soul moves ceaselessly upwards, always reviving its tension for its onward flight by means of the progress it has already realized. Indeed, it is only spiritual activity that nourishes its force by exercise; it does not slacken its tension by action but rather increases it."

Your desire for God is insatiable. You stretch out at every moment with burning desire to possess more of God, to be more penetrated by God's allness. You do reach some stage of resting in the Lord, but then the movement starts again. From light to shadow to darkness. You come back, as T.S. Eliot writes, to the beginning and see it for the first time. Your stability and grounding in God's infinite love is the beginning of motion toward greater perfection, the possession of God in greater consciousness. It is the motion toward greater love and promise of greater life of the Bride in *The Song of Songs*: "On my bed, at night, I sought him, whom my heart loves. I sought but did not find him. So I will rise and go through the city; in the streets and the squares I will seek him whom my heart loves" *(Song of Songs: 3:1-2)*

A STRETCHING TOWARD OTHERS

Your greater desire in life among all desires, your wisdom above all other knowledge, is to be more one with God, your Beloved. This is love experienced that begets love toward others. True contemplation is authenticated by the love you show toward others in humble service, for this alone—the acceptance of others in self-sacrificing love—proves that you have truly experienced a genuine love from the Source of all beauty and goodness. God's beauty becomes your participated beauty and such beauty always spreads itself outward, stretches toward others in loving gift. Contemplation that does not reap a harvest in shared love toward others is a deception and in the end is dehumanizing. A true contemplative is always begetting, becoming the other in greater unity of love as he/she stretches out to become *love*.

SPIRITUAL DIRECTION
Contemporary Readings   5.95

Edited by Kevin Culligan, O.C.D. The revitalized ministry of spiritual direction is one of the surest signs of renewal in today's Church. In this book seventeen leading writers and spiritual directors discuss history, meaning, demands and practice of this ministry. Readers of the book should include not just a spiritual elite, but the entire Church — men and women, clergy and laity, members of religious communities.

PRAYER:
The Eastern Tradition   2.95

Andrew Ryder, S.C.J. In the East there is no sharp distinction between prayer and theology. Far from being divorced they are seen as supporting and completing each other. One is impossible without the other. Theology is not an end in itself, but rather a means, a way to union with God.

THE RETURNING SUN
Hope for a Broken World   2.50

George A. Maloney, S.J. In this collection of meditations, the author draws on his own experiences rooted in Eastern Christianity to aid the reader to enter into the world of the "heart." It is hoped that through contemplation of this material he/she will discover the return of the inextinguishable Sun of the universe, Jesus Christ, in a new and more experiential way.

BREAD FOR THE EATING   2.95

Kelly B. Kelly. Sequel to the popular *Grains of Wheat*, this small book of words received in prayer draws the reader closer to God through the imagery of wheat being processed into bread. The author shares her love of the natural world.

LIVING HERE AND HEREAFTER
Christian Dying,
Death and Resurrection   2.95

Msgr. David E. Rosage. The author offers great comfort to us by dispelling our fears and anxieties about our life after this earthly sojourn. Based on God's Word as presented in Sacred Scripture, these brief daily meditations help us understand more clearly and deeply the meaning of suffering and death.

PRAYING WITH SCRIPTURE
IN THE HOLY LAND
Daily Meditations With the Risen Jesus   3.50

Msgr. David E. Rosage. Herein is offered a daily meeting with the Risen Jesus in those Holy Places which He sanctified by His human presence. Three hundred and sixty-five scripture texts are selected and blended with the pilgrimage experiences of the author, a retreat master, and well-known writer on prayer.

DISCERNMENT:
Seeking God in Every Situation   3.50

Rev. Chris Aridas. "Many Christians struggle with ways to seek, know and understand God's plan for their lives. This book is prayerful, refreshing and very practical for daily application. It is one to be read and used regularly, not just read" *(Ray Roh, O.S.B.).*

DISCOVERING
PATHWAYS TO PRAYER   .2.95

Msgr. David E. Rosage. Following Jesus was never meant to be dull, or worse, just duty-filled. Those who would aspire to a life of prayer and those who have already begun, will find this book amazingly thorough in its scripture-punctuated approach.

"A simple but profound book which explains the many ways and forms of prayer by which the person hungering for closer union with God may find him" *(Emmanuel Spillane, O.C.S.O., Abbot, Our Lady of the Holy Trinity Abbey, Huntsville, Utah).*

MOURNING: THE HEALING JOURNEY   2.95

Rev. Kenneth J. Zanca. Comfort for those who have lost a loved one. Out of the grief suffered in the loss of both parents within two months, this young priest has written a sensitive, sympathetic yet humanly constructive book to help others who have lost loved ones. This is a book that might be given to the newly bereaved.

THE BORN-AGAIN CATHOLIC   3.95

Albert H. Boudreau. This book presents an authoritative imprimatur treatment of today's most interesting religious issue. The author, a Catholic layman, looks at Church tradition past and present and shows that the born-again experience is not only valid, but actually is Catholic Christianity at its best. The exciting experience is not only investigated, but the reader is guided into revitalizing his or her own Christian experience. The informal style, colorful personal experiences, and helpful diagrams make this book enjoyable and profitable reading.

WISDOM INSTRUCTS HER CHILDREN
The Power of the Spirit and the Word   3.50

John Randall, S.T.D. The author believes that now is God's time for "wisdom." Through the Holy Spirit, "power" has become much more accessible in the Church. Wisdom, however, lags behind and the result is imbalance and disarray. The Spirit is now seeking to pour forth a wisdom we never dreamed possible. This outpouring could lead us into a new age of Jesus Christ! This is a badly needed, most important book, not only for the Charismatic Renewal, but for the whole Church.

GRAINS OF WHEAT   2.95

Kelly B. Kelly. This little book of words received in prayer is filled with simple yet often profound leadings, exhortations and encouragement for daily living. Within the pages are insights to help one function as a Christian, day by day, minute by minute.

LIVING FLAME PRESS
Box 74, Locust Valley, N.Y. 11560

QUANTITY

_____ Journey Into Contemplation—3.95

_____ Spiritual Direction—5.95

_____ The Returning Sun—2.50

_____ Prayer: the Eastern Tradition—2.95

_____ Living Here and Hereafter—2.95

_____ Praying With Scripture in the
Holy Land—3.50

_____ Discernment—3.50

_____ Mourning: The Healing Journey—2.95

_____ The Born-Again Catholic—3.95

_____ Wisdom Instructs Her Children—3.50

_____ Discovering Pathways to Prayer—2.95

_____ Grains of Wheat—2.95

_____ Bread for the Eating—2.95

NAME_____

ADDRESS_____

CITY_____ STATE_____ ZIP_____

Kindly include $.70 postage and handling on orders up to $5; $1.00 on
orders up to $10; more than $10 but less than $50, add 10% of total; over
$50, add 8% of total. Canadian residents add 20% exchange rate, plus
postage and handling. N.Y. State residents add 7% tax unless exempt.